MILTON

PRIVATE CORRESPONDENCE AND
ACADEMIC EXERCISES
·

LONDON
Cambridge University Press
FETTER LANE

NEW YORK · TORONTO
BOMBAY · CALCUTTA · MADRAS
Macmillan

TOKYO
Maruzen Company Ltd

MILTON

PRIVATE CORRESPONDENCE AND ACADEMIC EXERCISES

Translated from the Latin
by
PHYLLIS B. TILLYARD
Late Scholar of Girton College, Cambridge
Late Lecturer at Westfield and
East London Colleges

With an
Introduction & Commentary
by
E. M. W. TILLYARD
University Lecturer in English
Late Fellow of Jesus College
Cambridge

CAMBRIDGE
AT THE UNIVERSITY PRESS
1932

PRINTED IN GREAT BRITAIN

CONTENTS

v

CONTENTS

MILTON'S ACADEMIC EXERCISES

vi

PREFACE

MILTON'S *Prolusiones Oratoriae*, or Latin exercises composed to fulfil the academic requirements of Cambridge, although very uneven in their interest, are extremely important for what they tell us about Milton's university days and about his own character and ambitions. In the eighteenth century, when educated people could read Latin easily, they were known to serious students of Milton. Later, no one having troubled to translate them, they were gradually forgotten, till Masson called attention to their importance in the first volume of his *Life of Milton*. Since then, students of Milton have paid these *Prolusions* rather more heed, but certainly not as much as they deserve. Never having been translated and being omitted from the familiar Bohn edition of Milton's prose they simply do not come in most readers' way. The first object of this book is to make these *Prolusiones Oratoriae* accessible by a translation; and it is hoped thereby to fill a real gap in Milton scholarship.

Along with his *Prolusions*, Milton published his private correspondence in Latin. This, having been translated and being included in the Bohn edition of Milton's prose, is better known than the *Prolusions*. However, the translations are in various ways deficient, and a new rendering is undoubtedly needed. The whole of Milton's small volume, therefore, has been translated.

The text of this volume has been departed from in two ways only. The twenty-second letter (to Richard

Jones) has been restored to its proper place, the eighteenth, in the order of the letters, which is uniformly
(but for this one exception) chronological; and Milton's
poem *At a Vacation Exercise* has been printed at the end
of the *Sixth Prolusion*, of which it originally formed a
portion and apart from which it cannot be understood.

The introduction deals partly with the letters, but at
greater length with the *Prolusions*. Something is said
about Milton at Cambridge, but not outside what immediately concerns the *Prolusions*. The author has dealt
generally with Milton's life and writings during his
Cambridge years in his *Milton*, chaps. ii–v.

For the headings, *Prolusio Oratoria* has been translated *Academic Exercise*, as this phrase is more ex-
pressive than the shorter *Prolusion*. But *Prolusion* is
the more usual and convenient term and has been
preferred in the text.

Special thanks are due to Dr A. H. Lloyd, of Christ's
College, for his kindness in searching the college documents and thereby identifying the college servant whose
name plays so large a part in the *Sixth Prolusion*.

P. B. T.

E. M. W. T.

INTRODUCTION

I   THE TEXT

IN 1674, the year of Milton's death, Brabazon Aylmer, a printer of Cornhill, sought permission of the authorities to publish the public and private correspondence of Milton. To the private correspondence there was no objection, but the public correspondence consisted of letters of State, composed by Milton on behalf of the Cromwellian government for despatch to the various courts of Europe. The time had not yet come when anything to do with Cromwell could be taken calmly, and permission to publish Milton's public correspondence was denied. Thereupon the printer solicited Milton for something to take its place. Milton discovered in his papers some of the Latin exercises or disputations he had composed at Cambridge to satisfy the requirements for his degrees. The printer accepted these and published them along with Milton's private letters in a duodecimo volume.

This volume is the sole authority for the text of very nearly all the letters and of all the exercises. Besides being badly punctuated it contains not a few misprints, the most important of which are specified in the textual notes, but it is not more inaccurate than one would expect a printed Latin book dated 1674 to be. Subsequent editions have faithfully reproduced the original mistakes. Textually, therefore, it is the original edition only that counts.

2   MILTON'S PRIVATE CORRESPONDENCE

If the reader expects to find in Milton's letters the sort of thing that he finds in those of Howell or Lamb or Keats, he will be disappointed. He will also be misjudging Milton's intention. For Milton treated the

Latin letter as a serious set form of composition, on which a good deal of trouble had to be expended. It was something that served among other things to exhibit the writer's command over the Latin language. So it is that he apologises for possible deficiencies in a passage like the following:

I write this in London, among the distractions of the town, not, as usual, surrounded by books. So if anything in this letter fails to please you or to fulfil your expectations, it shall be made good in another, upon which more pains have been bestowed, as soon as I return to the haunts of the Muses.

Taking into account this presumption of rhetoric in Milton's letters, we can easily explain certain of their features. First, the long letters are invariably better than the short. Many of the best letter-writers charm us most when they have least to say. Not so Milton. Instead of allowing his fancy to fill the vacuum, he merely elaborates a few compliments or a few excuses for not having written before; and as the rhetorical virtuosity of such elaboration has ceased to charm, part of the reason for these letters' existence has disappeared. On the other hand, when Milton has matter to express and must needs write at length, he can write with urbanity or nobility: his rhetoric has found a function and we can enjoy it. Most of the long letters are good. Secondly, rhetoric helps, to explain a tone of formality which in some of the letters is rather distressing. In writing to a distinguished foreigner, Milton uses a mode of elegant hyperbole which is superbly appropriate. We at once understand why he had such a success in Italy. But when he is nearly as formal, without being so complimentary, in writing to an old pupil, our first thoughts are that Milton must have been rather disagreeable. Take these sentences from the thirtieth letter, to Richard Jones:

On no account allow yourself to imagine that I measure your gratitude (if indeed you owe me any) by the regularity of your letters. You can best prove your gratitude to me by showing the

results of those services of mine to you, of which you speak, not
so much in the frequency of your letters as in your steady devotion to noble pursuits and in the merits of your conduct.

This, we say, is tall stuff, little calculated to endear
Milton to his correspondent. Yet, if we remember the
presumption of rhetoric, we may somewhat revise our
opinions. To write tall stuff was part of the game. Milton
apparently had nothing particular to say to Jones; so he
played the game by filling out with a little rhetorical
moralising.

As examples of literary skill that still retains its
charm, I would cite letters twelve and twenty-three.
Philaras, to whom the first of these is addressed, by
birth an Athenian, educated in Italy, and a distinguished
scholar and diplomat, had admired Milton's *Defence of
the English People* against Salmasius and had written to
beg him to use his eloquence in the cause of freeing the
Greeks from Turkish rule. It is pretty plain from Milton's letter that he had no wish to accede to Philaras's
request, because he thought the Greeks of his time incapable of bearing the responsibilities of liberty. Yet
he succeeds in conveying this unpleasant opinion with
the most perfect urbanity, so delicately indeed that perhaps Philaras never consciously disentangled it from its
florid setting. (Milton, it may be remembered, somehow succeeded in including urbanity among the virtues
extracted from Scripture in the *De Doctrina Christiana*.)
More than half the letter consists of compliments: some
to Philaras, some to himself for having earned the praise
of anyone so distinguished as Philaras, a man in whom
all the lost virtues of ancient Greece have been revived.
The tone is perfect: it has a kind of baroque gravity like
that of a good heroic play; imperturbably and solemnly
exaggerated and yet critically conscious of the exaggera-
tion. Then Milton turns to the business in hand. Could
anything be more noble, more in keeping with classical
precedent, than to urge Europe to attempt the emanci-
pation of Greece? Yet what about the Greeks them-

selves? Should not *they* be first encouraged to emulate their ancestors? But you, Philaras, are the only person who can effect this. Doubtless *you* can do it; and when once it is done, the Greeks will be sufficient to themselves and other nations will stand by the Greeks. Nothing could be neater than the way Milton turns the tables on his correspondent.

The other letter, to Henry de Brass, is much simpler, containing no irony. It is a little essay on the nature of History and on Sallust as a historian. It is a beautiful piece of single-minded ardour culminating in the very Miltonic sentiment that only a man who is himself noble is qualified to write the actions of noble men.

One who would be a worthy historian of worthy deeds must possess as noble a spirit and as much practical experience as the hero of the action himself, in order that he may be able to comprehend and measure even the greatest of these actions on equal terms.

Such are some of Milton's qualities as a writer of letters. Something remains to be said of the letters, not as letters, but as documents telling us things about Milton. The intervals at which they were written are irregular. For instance, Milton left but one letter dating from after the Restoration and as many as twenty written in the decade before. His letters, therefore, cannot furnish us with a steady record of his life and development. Yet up to a point they are very valuable in showing us how he changed: they give us contrasted glimpses of him at different times.

First comes a group of four letters written when Milton was an undergraduate. They are stilted compositions and, except that they show a genuine affection for Young and the younger Gill, to whom they are addressed, they lack the more amiable qualities in Milton's nature which certain passages in the *Prolusions* and the *Nativity Ode* reveal in him at about this time. On the other hand they tell us (see the third letter) that Milton was disappointed with his fellow-undergraduates, disgusted with the superficiality of their learning and with the levity of many of them in becoming theologians with no proper basis of general knowledge. He longs to get away where he can bury himself in solitary and unbroken study. With the dons his standing must have been high, for he tells us that he has supplied one of them with some Latin verses, to be used at a University function.

After a long interval follow three letters of the Horton period. We now see Milton in the midst of the solitary and unbroken study he had longed for in his Cambridge days. The seventh letter, to Diodati, is an invaluable record of Milton's state of mind before he wrote *Lycidas*. In the vehement manner, the somewhat feverish Platonic tone in which he speaks of his friendship with Diodati, we may detect the strain on him of his unremitted studies at Horton, perhaps too of his resolve, deliberately taken five years before, to put off all idea of early marriage.

Ceres never sought her daughter Proserpine (as the legend tells) with greater ardour than I do this Idea of Beauty, like some image of loveliness; ever pursuing it, by day and by night, in every shape and form ("for many forms there are of things divine") and following close in its footprints as it leads. And so, whensoever I find one who spurns the base opinions of common men, and dares to be, in thought and word and deed, that which the wisest minds throughout the ages have approved; whensoever, I say, I find such a man, to him I find myself impelled forthwith to cleave.

But though there may be a sense of strain, ambition and the eagerness to be doing inform the letter.

What am I thinking about? you ask. So help me God, of immortality. What am I doing? Growing wings and learning to fly.

And the eagerness is not confined to the passages which deal with his ambitions; it has entered the texture of his prose, by now truly eloquent and far superior to the stilted rhetoric of his Cambridge letters.

Two letters survive from Milton's Italian tour, and a

third, written years later from England to his Florentine friend, Carlo Dati, may be associated with them. Of all the groups of the letters this gives the fullest, or at least the most agreeable, picture of Milton. The formality of style which in the Cambridge letters was unpleasantly cold and stilted now seems to glow with an apt Italianate warmth. The baroque of Lecce has, as it were, supplanted the baroque of Peterhouse chapel. This time the tone is exactly right. The candid delight Milton shows in the Italians' good opinion of him and the generous affection it provoked in return are charmingly expressed. To those who imagine that Milton was a bigoted Protestant it will be surprising to hear him praising Catholics so ardently; in particular Cardinal Barberini, Prime Minister of Rome, protector of the interests of England and Scotland at the Papal Court. And in his letter from England to Dati he is almost pathetically anxious that his anti-Catholic principles should not alienate his Catholic friends. Freedom of speech he must have; but he values his friends to the utmost and cannot relinquish them.

Except the above letter to Dati, none survives between 1639, the year Milton left Italy, and 1652, the period of the Salmasian controversy and the culmination of his blindness. But between the latter year and 1659 come twenty letters, or nearly two-thirds of Milton's total correspondence. In these years Milton was a man of international importance, much visited by foreigners. Aubrey tells us how "the only inducement of severall foreigners that came over into England, was chiefly to see Oliver Protector and Mr. J. Milton". Fifteen out of the twenty letters are written to foreigners; the other five to former pupils. The contents of the whole group are so miscellaneous that one can make no general comment. The letters to Philaras and Henry de Brass have been mentioned before. The second of these, it may be noted, is only one of several that show Milton's deep love of history. Perhaps the most interesting of all the group is the second letter to Philaras, concerning his blindness. It is famous as describing the symptoms, and has prompted numerous theories as to why Milton went blind. But it illustrates admirably his sensitiveness and his courage. He was proud of his own physical fitness, and had no sentimental liking for disease. This pride may help us to estimate the anguish behind his remark in this letter that his blindness may be causing many to regard him with feelings of contempt. But his courage blazes up higher still. He will not repine at God's will and he bids Philaras farewell "with as much courage and composure as if I had the eyes of Lynceus".

The single letter that post-dates the Restoration is of the first interest in revealing how severe the shock of that event must have been. The twenty-ninth letter, written in 1659, had shown Milton still confident in the future of his own political cause. When the blow fell it seems to have extinguished patriotism from his heart.

The virtue you call statesmanship (but which I would rather have you call loyalty to my country), after captivating me with her fair-sounding name, has, so to speak, almost left me without a country....One's country is wherever it is well with one.

This is the mood of *Paradise Regained*, with which Milton was occupied in the year this letter was written. Christ in that poem had meditated political action, the patriotic work of rescuing Israel from the Roman yoke;

> Yet held it more humane, more heavenly first
> By winning words to conquer willing hearts,
> And make perswasion do the work of fear.

Christ, the perfect man, did not need experience, as Milton did, to learn the futility of staking everything on political action. No letter survives to correspond with the qualified patriotism of *Samson Agonistes*.

Such are some of the features that make Milton's letters important to anyone interested in his life and character. I have left unmentioned many more of those features than I have had room here to discuss.

3 MILTON'S ACADEMIC EXERCISES

Milton's *Prolusions* or *Academic Exercises*, when understood, enrich our knowledge of what Cambridge was like in the years 1625 to 1632. But in order to understand them, a little previous knowledge of conditions in Cambridge is necessary.

The University was at that time in a very flourishing state. To quote the late Dr J. Venn:

Few persons have adequately realised the commanding position to which the two Universities had thus attained. Absolutely— not relatively merely—the number of graduates in the years about 1625–30 was greater than was ever attained again till within living memory. When allowance is made for growth of population, it must be frankly admitted that, as far as concerns the number of trained men sent out into the country, the Universities have not yet regained the position they occupied two centuries and a half ago.

The percentage of men, later to become distinguished, who passed through the Universities at that time must have been very high. Still, in numbers Cambridge was little more than half what it is now, and its life was incalculably narrower. Undergraduates came up several years younger, and remained in residence twice as long. The numbers passing through Cambridge would therefore be but a quarter of those passing through now. Communication with townsfolk was strenuously discouraged. The men lived close together in college, and their tutors were more like house-masters than like their present-day descendants. It was a small world in which everyone knew everyone else. The range of studies was comparatively narrow. All these conditions must have induced a strong self-centredness, an atmosphere of strenuous "shop", more usually associated with school than with University.

The discipline too, at least for those who had not yet got their B.A., was that of a school. Five o'clock was the hour for rising to attend morning chapel. Breakfast was at six. Then followed four hours' work. Dinner was eaten at noon. There was two hours' more work after dinner. Supper at seven was the only other fixture of the day. Though this routine has much of the school about it, the success with which discipline was preserved was very different from what is expected in a school to-day. Milton in his *Sixth Prolusion* refers to an excursion made by fifty third-year men to Barnwell Field where they appear to have attacked an aqueduct and cut off one of the local water-supplies. This would be but one of many troubles, and complaints reached the Government of the bad state of discipline at this time.

The education in Milton's Cambridge was still founded on the medieval system. The three-and-a-half years spent on gaining the B.A. degree were mainly devoted to Rhetoric, Logic, and Metaphysics. Latin and some Greek were taught along with these. Little Mathematics, no History or Science, were included in the course. Everything was supposed to lead up to the *Disputation*, a medieval legacy which took the place of the modern examination. To qualify for a degree every student had from time to time to maintain or to attack a given thesis before an audience, sometimes in his college, sometimes in the Public Schools of the University. It is some of these Exercises or Prolusions on set themes, composed by Milton to satisfy the requirements for his two degrees, that were saved and printed in the 16/4 volume.

Narrow as the education may seem, there is a good deal to be said for it, as actually put into practice in Milton's day. First, some latitude was allowed in choice of subject and in the way a subject was treated. History may not have been in the syllabus, yet it seems to have been quite legitimate to work history into a non-historical subject. Thus Milton, called on to defend the very scholastic thesis that "there are no partial forms in an animal in addition to the whole", works in a long disquisition on the decline of the Roman Empire. Given an enlightened tutor, an undergraduate might be able to indulge his tastes to a large extent. Second, the system of disputation ensured the dons having close contact with their pupils. They took part in the disputations themselves and had to teach their pupils to argue. Some idea of the opportunities a lucky undergraduate might have in Milton's day can be gathered from our knowledge of Joseph Meade, one of the tutors of Christ's. Meade (whose diary is the chief source of the details of Cambridge life in Milton's day) had extended his learning far beyond the range of subjects required for the usual degrees. He was versed in mathematics, modern languages, history, anatomy, and botany. He was also an extremely conscientious tutor, seeing his pupils every evening. This is how his biographer describes these interviews:

In the evening they all came to his chamber to satisfie him that they had performed the task he had set them. The first question he used to propound to every one in his order was: *Quid dubitas?* What doubts have you met in your studies to-day? For he supposed that to doubt nothing and to understand nothing were verifiable alike. Their doubts being propounded, he resolved their *Quaere's* and so set them upon clear ground to proceed more distinctly. And then having by prayer commended them and their studies to God's protection and blessing, he dismissed them to their lodgings.

Another advantage of the educational system was the actual practice of the public debates; quite apart from the subjects chosen. Habitual attendance at these functions must have sharpened the young men's wits; and a keen audience must have put the speakers on their mettle. Milton's *Prolusions* recreate for us very vividly the consciousness of the audience. We feel that this audience extracted things from Milton's mind which without it would have remained dormant: for example a certain kind of undergraduate wit. The wit may not be very brilliant, but it was good for Milton to have it forced from him. The debate was indeed admirably suited to intensifying and enlivening the narrow, self-centred, but active spirit of early seventeenth-century Cambridge.

This gives the good side of Cambridge education. The bad can be seen from the *Fourth* or *Fifth Prolusions* of Milton. In the former, Milton was called on to maintain that "in the destruction of any substance there can be no resolution into first matter". He conducts the argument in the strictest *a priori* manner of medieval philosophy. There is not the least hint that in a scientific matter experiment of any kind should be admitted. This *Prolusion* was typical of a large number, probably the large majority of the University exercises. Whatever value this scholastic method may have had in exercising the brain it implied that Cambridge at that period officially ignored the recent revolution in mathematical and scientific thought. If for Donne the new philosophy had called all in doubt it had entirely failed to penetrate the ears of those in authority at Cambridge. To a young man eager to learn the changes in thought and the new discoveries of science it must have been agony to be kept for years to the treadmill of scholastic logic.

However, though official education was medieval, there existed within the University a party of reformers. Of this party Milton's *Prolusions* are some of the chief evidence. Its inspiration was Francis Bacon. Years before at Cambridge, Bacon had revolted against the methods of teaching, the subservience to Aristotle interpreted medievally. As his earliest biographer said,

He fell into the dislike of the philosophy of Aristotle; not for the worthlessness of the author, to whom he would ever ascribe high attributes, but for the unfruitfulness of the way.

Three years before Milton's birth, in 1605, Bacon vented this dislike in various passages of the *Advancement of Learning*. The chief subject of University education he condemns as "vain matter".

Surely, like as many substances in nature which are solid do putrify and corrupt into worms, so it is the property of good and sound knowledge to putrify and dissolve into a number of subtile, idle, unwholesome, and (as I may term them) vermiculate questions, which have indeed a kind of quickness and life of spirit, but no soundness of matter or goodness of quality. This kind of degenerate learning did chiefly reign amongst the schoolmen; who having sharp and strong wits, and abundance of leisure, and small variety of reading; but their wits being shut up in the cells of a few authors (chiefly Aristotle their dictator), as their persons were shut up in the cells of monasteries and colleges; and knowing little history, either of nature or time; did out of no great quantity of matter, and infinite agitation of wit, spin out unto us those laborious webs of learning which are extant in their books.

In another place Bacon advocates a complete overhaul of University teaching.

Although the *Advancement of Learning* produced no effect on the academic authorities, Bacon was far too diplomatic to take offence. He took the greatest care to keep on good terms with his University, without ceasing to plead for reform. In 1620 he presented a copy of his *Novum Organum* to the University with a letter, deferential in tone but calling attention to the new method propounded in his work. Again, in 1623 he presented a copy of the *De Argumentis Scientiarum* with the following address:

To

THE UNIVERSITY OF CAMBRIDGE

The debts of a son, such as I can, I discharge. And what I do myself, I exhort you to do likewise; that is to apply yourselves strenuously to the advancement of the sciences, in modesty of mind to retain liberty of understanding, and not to lay up in a napkin the talent which has been transmitted to you in trust from the ancients. Surely the grace of the divine light will attend and shine upon you, if humbling and submitting Philosophy to Religion you make a legitimate and dexterous use of the keys of the senses; and putting away all zeal of contradiction, each dispute with other as if he were disputing with himself. Farewell.

Zeal of contradiction is plainly a hit at the *Disputation* with its endless raising of objections and counter-objections. Finally, by his will Bacon left money to found a lectureship in history, a subject dear to his heart and completely neglected at Cambridge. Unfortunately, when he died in 1626, the money was found not to be there, and the lectureship never came into being.

The authority of Bacon must have given the reforming party in Cambridge some strength, but that their position was not easy is shown by the following incident. Shortly after Bacon's death, Lord Brooke, himself influenced by Bacon's teaching, founded a lectureship in history at Cambridge. The holder could not be a cleric, and might be a foreigner. As no Englishman could be found qualified for the post (the study of history being at a very low ebb in this country), Isaac Dorislaus of Leyden was appointed. He gave his first lecture in December 1627. Unfortunately some political references in it gave offence to Wren, the High Church Master of Peterhouse. Wren wrote to Laud, who caused Dorislaus to be forbidden to lecture. The unlucky Dutchman, completely innocent of wishing to give offence, made humble apology. He became the centre of contending factions. The ban was removed, reimposed, removed again; but finally Lord Brooke invited him to give up Cambridge and join his household. Dorislaus was glad to accept the offer. It is quite clear from the incident that a strong section of the authorities were bitterly hostile to any educational reform. And we may guess that the feelings of the reformers were correspondingly violent.

Such were some of the features of the Cambridge which Milton entered in 1625. How Milton reacted to it we know pretty clearly from the *Prolusions*, the letters, a few passages in his Latin poems and later pamphlets, and from one or two remarks by his biographers. His academic record was unimpeachable. "Was a very hard student in the University", said Aubrey, "and performed all his exercises there with very good applause." But he quarrelled with his first tutor, was for two years at least unpopular with most of his fellow-undergraduates, was actively opposed to the prevailing system of education, and for years afterwards continued to express that opposition. Indeed Cambridge seems to have evoked all those powers of resistance which in a congenial home and at a school where his talents were appreciated had been quiescent. It is quite possible that the whole trouble arose from his declaring from the first for the Baconians or educational reformers. His tutor Chappell was an exceptionally skilful disputant, presumably a strong believer in the prevailing system. Milton, exasperated at having to spend time on scholastic subtleties when he wanted to study history or mathematics, probably gave his candid opinion on educational methods. And no wonder there was trouble. When, in his *First Prolusion*, he mentions the undergraduates' hostility, he speaks of the rivalry of those who pursue different studies, as if the quarrel was educational rather than personal:

How can I hope for your good-will, when in all this great assembly I encounter none but hostile glances, so that my task seems to be to placate the implacable? So provocative of animosity, even in the home of learning, is the rivalry of those who pursue different studies or whose opinions differ concerning the studies they pursue in common....Yet to prevent complete despair, I see here and there, if I do not mistake, some who without a word show clearly by their looks how well they wish me.

It is to the credit both of Cambridge and of Milton that these rivalries admitted of reconciliation. Milton was transferred to a more congenial tutor; and in the *Sixth Prolusion*, or *Vacation Exercise*, he refers most generously to his late opponents, now reconciled to him. The fact is that though freedom of speech was a necessity of his nature, he was singularly free from personal rancour, having a sweetness of disposition difficult at first sight to reconcile with the violence of some of his utterances. And freedom of speech the authorities were wise enough to allow him, for the *Third Prolusion* is a direct attack on the Scholastic Philosophy, indeed on the whole educational system of Cambridge.

The date of this composition is uncertain, but cannot be very far removed from the time when, as described above, Dorislaus retired from Cambridge owing to the action of Laud. As Milton expressly speaks of the importance of history, his speech must have stirred up feeling pretty effectively. It is interesting to note that two or three years after this *Prolusion* a certain Nicholas Ganning, Fellow of Corpus, was "objected to as a disputant at the Commencement of 1631 on the ground that he railed against school divinity, whereas King James and King Charles commanded young students in divinity to begin with Lombard and Aquinas". In tone Milton's *Prolusion* is entirely uncompromising. It is less an argument than a glowing poetical denunciation of scholastic philosophy and a panegyric of the new studies advocated by Bacon. This is how he describes the studies he hates:

When I go through these empty quibbles as I often must, against my will, it seems to me as if I were forcing my way through rough and rocky wastes, desolate wildernesses, and precipitous mountain gorges. And so it is not likely that the dainty and elegant Muses preside over these ragged and tattered studies, or consent to be the patrons of their maudlin partisans; and I cannot believe that there was ever a place for them on Parnassus unless it were some waste corner at the very foot of the mountain, some spot with naught to commend it, tangled and matted with thorns and brambles, overgrown with thistles and nettles, remote from the dances and company of the goddesses, where no laurels grow nor flowers bloom, and to which the sound of Apollo's lyre can never penetrate.

And when he praises the studies of his choice, the prose rises to a pitch of enthusiasm unequalled by any of his verse written at that date.

But how much better were it, gentlemen, and how much more consonant with your dignity, now to let your eyes wander as it were over all the lands depicted on the map, and to behold the places trodden by the heroes of old, to range over the

xxiii

regions made famous by wars, by triumphs, and even by the tales of poets of renown, now to traverse the stormy Adriatic, now to climb unharmed the slopes of fiery Etna, then to spy out the customs of mankind and those states which are well-ordered; next to seek out and explore the nature of all living creatures, and after that to turn your attention to the secret virtues of stones and herbs. And do not shrink from taking your flight into the skies and gazing upon the manifold shapes of the clouds, the mighty piles of snow, and the source of the dews of morning; then inspect the coffers wherein the hail is stored and examine the arsenals of the thunderbolts. And do not let the intent of Jupiter or of Nature elude you, when a huge and fearful comet threatens to set the heavens aflame, nor let the smallest star escape you of all the myriads which are scattered and strewn between the poles: yes, even follow close upon the sun in all his journeys, and ask account of time itself and demand the reckoning of its eternal passage.

Even when forced to engage in the scholastic game he does not give up the battle. In the *Fourth Prolusion* he punctuates his dialectic with the remark that he expects he is boring his hearers as he is certainly boring himself. And in the *Fifth Prolusion* he drags a long disquisition on Roman history into a purely scholastic topic—history being one of the subjects he was most anxious should supplant the scholastic philosophy.

Interesting for the history of education as are Milton's attacks on surviving medievalism, they are still more so for what they tell us about himself. They show him, long before his first pamphleteering days at the beginning of the Civil War, as the young reformer, naïvely trusting in a root-and-branch policy, too little suspicious of the insensibility of human nature, and over-confident in the power of rules and institutions to hasten or delay an Age of Gold.

Such then is the way in which Milton reacted to the educational system at Cambridge, as shown especially in the *Third Prolusion*. The other *Prolusions* may now be examined in turn for anything of note they tell us about Milton and his university life.

It is unfortunate that only one of the *Prolusions* is

dated. This is the *Vacation Exercise*, delivered in the
Long Vacation. The verses *At a Vacation Exercise*, which
originally accompanied it, Milton tells us were written
when he was nineteen. The exercise dates then in the
summer of 1628, Milton's fourth year of college. From
the references, quoted above, to academic rivalry, the
First Prolusion ante-dates the *Vacation Exercise*. The
elaborate *Seventh Prolusion*, on Learning and Ignorance, is obviously the maturest of all. It also suggests
that Milton had already embarked on the comprehensive voyage of discovery pursued at Horton. Masson
is probably right, therefore, in thinking it Milton's last
College exercise before he left Cambridge in July 1632.
The *Second Prolusion*, on the Harmony of the Spheres,
so closely resembles the *Nativity Ode* that I should date
it about 1629. For the dates of the other three there is
practically no evidence.

The *First Prolusion*, delivered in mid-winter, concerned the appropriate question whether day or night
were the more excellent. Milton does not take the subject very seriously; he is half bored. So he plays with it,
pads it out elaborately with mythology, indulges in
some very youthful jokes, salts it with a little irony, and
every now and then, being Milton, cannot prevent his
imagination from shooting up. The classical mythology,
tedious to most modern readers, must have been appreciated in Milton's day. It was common ground, much
of it, to every one in the audience; it brought with it
the delightful sense of familiarity within the academic
clique and of strangeness and bafflement without it. It
ministered to the vanity of a compact self-centred community. And Milton's classical mythology, well based
on the familiar legends to reassure the majority, was in
part learned and remote enough to add a flavour of
novelty. His jokes are engagingly simple. For instance
in discussing the mythologists and what they made of
the old legends of the parentage and alliances of Night
and Day he says:

But why they should believe that Phanes, endowed as he was with a wondrous and superhuman beauty, was so much in love with Night, a mere mulatto or silhouette, as even to wish to marry her, seems a problem hopelessly difficult to solve, unless the phenomenal scarcity of females at that time left him no choice.

More engaging, and surprising to those who think Milton incapable of being witty or critical at his own expense, is the sudden bathos after his highest flight. In praising the beauty of Day, he breaks into a poetical description of the dawn. The beasts rejoice, the flowers open their petals to the sun,

the Earth too decks herself in lovelier robes to honour the Sun's coming, and the clouds, arrayed in garb of every hue, attend the rising god in festive train and long procession.

Mankind in different parts of the world greet the rising sun with pomp and sacrifice—and, to you, gentlemen, of all men is the sun most welcome, for he allows you to get back to your studies so cruelly interrupted by the inclemency of night. It is all very obvious and sweet and simple-minded, but there is considerable pleasure in seeing the redoubtable Milton showing these of all qualities. In sum this *Prolusion*, callow and "shoppy" though it is, has somehow the quality of charm. It re-creates the picture of a very young man, of powerful, ardent, but generous and responsive nature, set in a society which was curiously confined but by no means lacked character and vitality.

In point of sheer craft the *Second Prolusion*, on the harmony of the spheres, is the best of them all. And one may easily miss the craft in the apparent lightness with which the theme is treated. When we read Milton on the music of the spheres we expect sublimity; when we do not find sublimity, we are only too apt to stop expecting anything at all. It is a little difficult to realise that Milton was ever capable of treating such a subject wittily or with urbanity. Not that there is no sublimity in the piece, but as in the *First Prolusion*, though here far more elegantly, Milton curbs his flight with bathos and never allows sublimity to spoil the prevailing tone of the whole. There is a second reason, unconnected with the idea of what we expect from Milton, which explains why a modern can easily miss the excellence of this *Prolusion*: the recent decline of rhetoric. Now a condition of rhetoric is the assumption that there resides a virtue in the manner of statement apart from the theme that is being treated; that a theme may merely be the excuse for artifice or ornament or some extrinsic emotion. Many people are willing to allow a corresponding license in verse: they do not unreservedly agree with Arnold that in poetry "all depends on the subject. Choose a fitting action, penetrate yourself with the feeling of its situations; this done, everything else will follow". But the same people who allow something very like rhetoric in verse often cannot be so tolerant of prose. Prose to them exists for what it states, not for any game of artifice. All one can answer is that at certain periods rhetoric has actually meant a great deal to people, and that it should be possible to project oneself into one of those periods. If one can open one's mind to the idea that through a rhetorical framework a variety of experience can be expressed, it is easy to accomplish this feat. And once the feat is accomplished one hesitates to limit very strictly the range of experience with which rhetoric can cope. Now the *Second Prolusion* of Milton is a piece of rhetoric. It is a short piece composed as a prologue to a set disputation; and there is no reason to suppose that Milton at that time was especially interested in the subject. He had to write on this subject, because the subject was there. What matters is the quality of rhetoric with which he treats the subject.

Milton develops his theme as follows. (It must be remembered that a knowledge of what Plato and Aristotle had to say about the music of the spheres was taken for granted in his audience.) He makes it clear that this *Prolusion* is a light prologue to a more rigorous discussion. And he carries out his intention by hovering delightfully between seriousness and banter. First, he says, Pythagoras and Plato never meant their theory of celestial music to be taken literally; it was but a poetical allegory. Aristotle, therefore, was unjust in attacking the literal doctrine. Indeed he deliberately misunderstood it thus in order to gain credit by demolishing the absurdity. And then Milton suddenly turns, and says—supposing for a moment the notion is taken literally, supposing the moving spheres are held to produce actual sounds, can we put up a defence? Perhaps after all the notion *is* true. Certainly nothing but exquisite music could have made the appalling dullness prevailing in the Aristotelian aether tolerable; without music it would have collapsed. Then he turns to deal with the objection that there can be no celestial music because no one on earth has ever heard it; and for a moment he touches on ideas about which he was extremely serious. Under the guise of Greek mythology he speaks of the age of innocence, of Adam, of the Fall, of Christ and possible regeneration. Once, he says, men could hear the music, but since Prometheus brought sin and degradation into the world by the theft of fire, they have fallen too low to apprehend it; in the words of the poet Milton may have had in mind as he wrote,

> But whilst this muddy vesture of decay
> Doth grossly close us in, we cannot hear it.

Pythagoras indeed may have heard it, but he perhaps was really a god. Then Milton adds something of his own. If only our souls were pure and chaste, like Pythagoras's, we could hear this music; and once we heard it, the Age of Gold would return. With a sudden and deliberate fall he ends by saying that his own unmelodious style has been offending against the very music of which he has been speaking. He had better stop.

This coupling of the music of the spheres with the Golden Age clearly associates the *Prolusion* with two verses (13 and 14) of the Hymn in the *Nativity Ode*.

Ring out ye Crystall sphears,
Once bless our human ears,
  (If ye have power to touch our senses so)
And let your silver chime
Move in melodious time;
    And let the Base of Heav'ns deep Organ blow,
And with your ninefold harmony
Make up full consort to th'Angelike symphony.

For if such holy Song
Enwrap our fancy long,
  Time will run back, and fetch the age of gold,
And speckl'd vanity
Will sicken soon and die,
    And leprous sin will melt from earthly mould,
And Hell it self will pass away,
    And leave her dolorous mansions to the peering day.

In the fourth chapter of my *Milton* I have discussed the *Nativity Ode*, noting its variety unique in Milton's poetry, the surprising and successful way in which it blends fancy and imagination. The *Second Prolusion* is of course a much smaller affair than the *Nativity Ode*, but the quality of its rhetoric links it with that poem. Milton blends banter and bathos and sublimity and dreams of a better world, with a success of which later in life he seems to have lost the art.

The *Third Prolusion*, against scholastic philosophy, has been dealt with above. But it is worth noticing how closely in its enthusiam for learning it resembles Milton's greater *Prolusion*, the seventh. The enthusiasm of its tone belongs to the Renaissance. Milton speaks of letting the mind go out on adventures:

Let not your mind rest content to be bounded and cabined by the limits which encompass the earth, but let it wander beyond the confines of the world.

He was to repeat the idea later: in *Areopagitica*, "minds that can wander beyond limit and satiety", and in the second book of *Paradise Lost*, "thoughts that wander through eternity". Milton's enthusiasm in the *Third Prolusion* is much like that of the youthful Marlowe. It is quite possible that in the above passages he was remembering unconsciously a famous passage from *Tamburlaine*:

> Nature, that fram'd us of four elements,
> Warring within our breasts for regiment,
> Doth teach us all to have aspiring minds:
> Our souls, whose faculties can comprehend
> The wondrous architecture of the world,
> And measure every wand'ring planet's course,
> Still climbing after knowledge infinite,
> And always moving as the restless spheres,
> Wills us to wear ourselves, and never rest.

Of the two next *Prolusions*, the rigidly scholastic disputations, I am not competent to speak. Only an expert in medieval philosophy could find them interesting in themselves or judge of their merits as philosophical exercises. But they have a secondary interest in showing us the sort of stuff Milton was attacking and in proving that his hostility was not due to his being unable to cope with the studies he attacked.

The *Sixth Prolusion*, or *Vacation Exercise*, was delivered after the end of the summer term of 1628. It is an elaborately comic entertainment celebrating the break-up of the year's serious studies. That Milton was chosen to give it—before almost the entire University, as he tells us—proves that he was by this time a popular and respected person. It consists of three parts. First an address on the theme that "sportive exercises on occasion are not inconsistent with philosophical studies". This is a kind of defence of the second part, which is entirely comic, a medley of hyperbole, topical references, and some bawdry. At the end of this part Milton introduces himself as the Father of the ten Aristotelian Predicaments and proceeds to the third part, the *Lines at a Vacation Exercise*, hitherto printed separately among the poems. It is a fragment of a kind of scholastic masque, with Milton as Ens, father of the ten Predicaments. The verses were supplemented by prose, presumably not written by Milton, which has not survived.

What makes the *Sixth Prolusion* so strange a production is that Milton was doing something for which he was quite unfitted yet of which through sheer force of will he made something of a success. It is plain that he took on the task not of his own choice but simply to oblige. He candidly admits that he has no aptitude for exuberant fun, and guards himself from misunderstanding by saying that any smut in which he indulges will spring not from himself but from the exigencies of the occasion. In the first part he fills up his deficiency in humorous matter by confiding to his audience with typical candour and simple-mindedness his own plans for self-education. Then he praises the eminence of his audience with the tallest rhetorical tautology. In a way he is noble and generous; but the tone is wrong, he strains himself too much for urbanity, and deviates into mere youthful bombast. Finally he defends mirth with an overwhelming series of arguments from reason, experience, and ancient example, all in the best Renaissance tradition. In a way Milton makes a hopeless mess of his task: nothing could be less fitting to a comic occasion than this mixture of redundant compliment and rhetorical argumentation. Yet for all that, as we read, we get caught up by the author's vitality. He forces us to pay him heed, however frigid the convention he makes use of. Moreover a fundamental charm breaks dimly through the superficial heaviness, as the flicker of a smile may transform a solemn face.

In the second part (chiefly famous for its allusion to Milton's nick-name of "the Lady") there was no escaping the duty of being funny, and Milton plunges headlong into his task. It is a queer, violent, breathless piece of work, in which the author's power of compulsion somehow succeeds in imposing itself on us. When he gets hold of a joke he pushes it with all the strength of his nature to fantastic lengths. For instance two of the college servants at Christ's had names that lent themselves to jokes about fires[1]; and flames, sparks, and embers fill several pages. And there is little doubt that the speaker by sheer vitality left his audience no choice but to respond.

It is easy to see why Milton added the verses. Only too conscious that in his comic prose he was doing something for which he had no aptitude, pride must have prompted him to give his audience a taste of what he could do; and he urges his verse to mount when he speaks of the "graver subjects" on which he would like to use it,

> Such where the deep transported mind may soare
> Above the wheeling poles, and at Heav'ns dore
> Look in, and see each blissful Deitie
> How he before the thunderous throne doth lie,
> Listening to what unshorn *Apollo* sings
> To th'touch of golden wires, while *Hebe* brings
> Immortal Nectar to her Kingly Sire.

As a whole, then, the *Vacation Exercise* is a strange medley of crudity, charm, simple-mindedness, and power. When we remember that its author was but nineteen, it is an impressive production. Further it gives, even more clearly than the *First Prolusion*, a picture of the self-centred active community that Cambridge was in the early years of Charles I.

The *Seventh Prolusion*, on the theme that Learning brings more blessings to men than Ignorance, is in an entirely different class from any of the other *Prolusions*, indeed from anything included in the 1674 volume. It is one of Milton's major works, and that it is almost unknown and has never before been translated in full is a reproach to Miltonic scholarship. It may not be comparable as a work of art to *L'Allegro* and *Il Penseroso* or to *Comus*, but in it Milton speaks out more fully and whole-heartedly than in any writing before *Lycidas*;

[1] For the identification of one of these, see note on p. 140.

and unless we give it the fullest heed we are apt to be completely mistaken about what Milton was doing with himself during his years of retirement at Horton. It is in this *Prolusion* that we have a full declaration of the vast ambitions that had possessed Milton and of his intention to promote them by acquiring an equipment of almost universal knowledge. He does not make an explicit declaration, but there is not the slightest doubt that when he speaks generally of the rewards which Learning may hope for, it is his own future that he has mainly in mind. It is remarkable how many ideas, well known in Milton's later works, are found fully formed or in embryo in this *Prolusion*. Much of the Miltonic philosophy can be gathered from it. Finally it is a superb piece of writing. The Latin has disengaged itself from the trammels of academic rhetoric and rises and falls with the ease and sweep of accomplished eloquence.

I can best point out the important details in the *Prolusion* by giving a brief summary of its argument.

First comes an elaborately argued exordium, a splendid piece of rhetoric, full of the joy of technical accomplishment. Milton, in the confiding manner we should now be used to, tells the audience of his ambition to acquire a full circle of knowledge and of his joys last summer when he retired to the country to study. Back at college he had hoped to continue his work, but he was called on to compose an oration on the advantages of Learning over Ignorance. To comply meant interrupting his course of Learning; and in anger he proposed to defend Ignorance, not subject to these interruptions. But fortune decided otherwise. Ignorance found her champion elsewhere, and Milton decides that he will be like a lover, forcibly separated from his true mistress, Learning, but getting comfort from singing her praises.

His main argument is inspired (if it is necessary to seek specific inspiration) by Plato and Bacon's *Advancement of Learning*. The human mind has in it a divine spark which, like one of the twin horses in the *Phaedrus*, struggles to mount upwards. It is Learning alone that aids this spark to succeed in its object and the mind to triumph over the body. To know the nature of things encourages the soul in its search after God, for when it examines the stars and the other wonders of the world it sees that they were created not for man's benefit but to proclaim God's glory. Perhaps Milton is here echoing a famous passage from Montaigne's *Apology of Raymond de Sebonde*. Compare this of Milton—

> Can we indeed believe, my hearers, that the vast spaces of boundless air are illuminated and adorned with everlasting lights, that these are endowed with such rapidity of motion and pass through such intricate revolutions, merely to serve as a lantern to base and slothful men?

with this from Montaigne (in Florio's version)—

> Who hath perswaded man, that this admirable moving of heavens vaults; that the eternal light of these lampes so fiercely rowling over his head; that the horror-moving and continuall motion of this infinite vaste Ocean, were established, and continue so many ages for his commoditie and service?[1]

Milton now raises and settles a possible argument against Learning. How is it that many ignorant men have been virtuous, many learned men vicious? The answer is that the power of learning only shows itself in one who is virtuous as well as learned. Such a man has an influence greater than that possessed by a host of ordinary mortals. Milton in this passage has two ideas at the back of his mind: first, the Renaissance exaltation of the great individual, possibly in its Calvinistic form,

---

[1] Here is another possible link between Montaigne and Milton. Phillips records that when Milton was living in London shortly after his return from Italy he would punctuate his austere and frugal life once in three weeks or a month with a gaudy-day. Was he acting on this passage from Montaigne (*Essais*, II, 2, *De l'Yvrognerie*)? "J'ay ouy dire à Silvius, excellent médicin de Paris, que, pour garder que les forces de nostre estomac ne s'aparessent, il est bon, une fois le mois, les esveiller par cet excez, et les picquer pour les garder de s'engourdir." But more probably Milton believed in the moral rather than the physical benefits of an occasional gaudy-day.

the insistence on the Elect; second, his own ambitions.
He will make himself one of these great men who influence the destinies of thousands. A passage of this
sort (it is one of several in this *Prolusion*) has an important bearing on the nature of Milton's prose works. It
is usually thought that Milton's early ambition was to
be a poet; that the prose works were undertaken entirely against his will, and that without the special
occasions that evoked them they would not have been
written. But this *Prolusion* suggests that Milton's
ambitions were very comprehensive. He wished to
sway men, to be a great teacher. Now at the end of the
autobiographical passage in the *Defensio Secunda* he
speaks of his earlier pamphlets as if they were a syste-
matic exposition of the idea of liberty in the various
spheres of life. And though actually these pamphlets
were occasioned by specific political or domestic events,
there is no reason to doubt Milton's statement that they
embody a coherent mass of teaching on which he had
pondered long before he committed it to print. It seems
to me quite clear that, in this *Seventh Prolusion*, Milton
is thinking of ambitions that were realised in the prose
works quite as much as of those that were realised in
Paradise Lost.

Next, Milton argues that if all learning is banished,
stark savagery must prevail. And to support his thesis
he gives a gross travesty (in the Renaissance-Protestant
manner) of the conditions of life in the Middle Ages.
Then he discusses the relation of the Intellect and the
Will. It is true that though the Intellect is the seat of
Learning, the Will is the parent of virtue. Yet the In-
tellect is the superior, for only by nourishment from the
Intellect can the Will exercise its proper function. The
Will is the agent, the Intellect the originator.

Having spoken generally, Milton deals with the influence of Learning on ordinary life; first private, then
public. This is the most important passage in the *Prolusion*. It is here that all Milton's ardour for knowledge

and the power of his personal ambitions break out. The extraordinary thing is that the whole spirit of this passage is not that of the soberer Neo-classic pursuit of detailed scientific knowledge but of the boundless expectations of the full Renaissance. Milton indeed writes like Marlowe, and as if the passionate disillusion which blighted those high hopes in the early seventeenth century had never existed. Past such a work as Donne's *Anniversaries*, past Webster with such sentiments as—

> Thou art happy, that thou hast not understanding
> To know thy misery: For all our wit
> And reading, brings us to a truer sense
> Of Sorrow—

Milton goes back and recaptures the simple expansive faith in the joys of knowledge, the insatiable appetite of the human mind, to be found in Marlowe and Sidney. He enumerates the transcendent prizes that reward Learning. It fortifies the mind against death. It promotes the highest form of friendship, even though it may rob a man of the superficial social graces. (Milton, it must be remembered, was never anti-social, and he consistently exalted the political as well as the individual virtues. Here he says that "the chief part of human happiness is derived from the society of one's fellows and the formation of friendships".) Then he launches out into a wonderful account of the universal cycle of knowledge, which he has confessed he is ambitious to complete. It goes through all the phenomena of the natural world to the soul of man and the nature of angels and demons. When this universal cycle of knowledge has been compassed, the spirit of man breaks from its prison-house and tramples on the shifting chances of life. He has become a kind of god, and has dominion over nature.

So at length, when universal learning has once completed its cycle, the spirit of man, no longer confined within this dark prison-house, will reach out far and wide, till it fills the whole world and the space far beyond with the expansion of its divine greatness.

Then at last most of the chances and changes of the world will be so quickly perceived that to him who holds this stronghold of wisdom hardly anything can happen in his life which is unforeseen or fortuitous. He will indeed seem to be one whose rule and dominion the stars obey, to whose command earth and sea hearken, and whom winds and tempests serve; to whom, lastly, Mother Nature herself has surrendered, as if indeed some god had abdicated the throne of the world and entrusted its rights, laws, and administration to him as governor.

Such was the quality of Milton's ambition. The passage is an amazing outburst of *hubris*, and, one would think, the product of a man inevitably doomed to disaster, obsessed by the illusions of the tragic hero, by the mood in which "the dove will peck the estridge". It seems incredible that a man who thought so overweeningly should have survived the humiliation of his first marriage—all his learning powerless to prevent an elementary social blunder—and the disappointment of the political hopes with which he had identified all his personal ambitions. The extraordinary thing about Milton was that somewhere in him was a humility that co-existed with this overweeningness and which saved him when disaster came. To gauge the extremes of Milton's nature, and with them its splendid scope, one should compare this hubristic passage from the *Seventh Prolusion* with Adam's words to Michael in the Twelfth Book of *Paradise Lost*, after he has witnessed the future history of the world.

> How soon hath thy prediction, Seer blest,
> Measur'd this transient World, the Race of time,
> Till time stand fixt: beyond is all abyss,
> Eternitie, whose end no eye can reach.
> Greatly instructed I shall hence depart,
> Greatly in peace of thought, and have my fill
> Of knowledge, what this vessel can containe;
> Beyond which was my folly to aspire.
> Henceforth I learne, that to obey is best,
> And love with feare the onely God, to walk
> As in his presence, ever to observe
> His providence, and on him sole depend,

Merciful over all his works, with good
Still overcoming evil, and by small
Accomplishing great things, by things deemd weak
Subverting worldly strong, and worldly wise
By simply meek.

Here Milton seems utterly to repudiate the appetite for boundless knowledge. Yet we should be as mistaken to accept this repudiation completely as we should be to conclude from the passage in the *Seventh Prolusion* that he was without all reason and humility. Overweeningness and humility, egotism and self-abnegation *always* co-existed in him. That he was ready, if necessary, at any moment to repress his self added power to his ambitions, while his humilities could never have been so impressive without the underlying potentiality of vast expansion.

There is an enthusiastic section on history and geography. History procures for its devotees a kind of retrospective immortality. When, next, Milton describes the honours with which great learning is rewarded he breaks out into fresh enthusiasm and again betrays his own ambitions:

To be the oracle of many nations, to find one's home regarded as a kind of temple, to be a man whom kings and states invite to come to them, whom men from near and far flock to visit, while to others it is a matter for pride if they have but set eyes on him once. These are the rewards of study, these are the prizes which learning can and often does bestow upon her votaries in private life.

It is pleasant to think that this ambition was at least partially fulfilled when Milton's replies to Salmasius had brought him an international fame.

In public life, Milton admits, the rewards of learning are fewer. The learned "enjoy a kingdom in themselves far more glorious than any earthly dominion"; and they cannot expect the double sway. (So early does Milton mention the idea of the "paradise within" happier than any external paradise, spoken of near the end of *Paradise*

Lost.) Yet the very greatest, Alexander and Augustus, were philosophers as well as statesmen.

If Ignorance raises the objection to Learning that life is short but Art long, the answer is to deny the proverb. It is our own slackness and our faulty methods of teaching the Arts that are wrong. This passage exhibits Milton's furiously active nature. It also foreshadows the main reason for the Fall in *Paradise Lost.* Eve ate the fruit not so much because she was greedy or disobedient as because she was too slack to realise the importance of the issue. The passage about education contains the germ of his later pamphlet on that subject. If only our methods were right, our trouble would be the opposite of what it is now: far from complaining that life is too short we should learn so much and so quickly that like Alexander we should sigh for more worlds to conquer.

Then he touches on the question of glory. Why labour to gain glory by Learning, says Ignorance, when the world may have but few more years to run and there may be too little time left in which men can glorify those to whom glory is due? His answer is the essence of *Lycidas*: "to have no thought of glory when we do well is above all glory". Moreover, there is heavenly glory, which matters far more than earthly. Those who have lived sparely and pursued the noble arts will be exalted in heaven.

He ends with an attack on the pleasures of Ignorance. They are at best but negative, ignoble and sheltered joys. They are unworthy even of beasts, even of inanimate things. Ignorance would degrade us below the very stocks and stones.

Such in outline is Milton's *Seventh Prolusion*. It may be arrogant in parts, and it may be too rhetorical for modern tastes, but it is one of Milton's major works and one of the noblest expressions of the enthusiasm for Learning that held men's minds in the full tide of the Renaissance.

PRIVATE
CORRESPONDENCE
&
ACADEMIC EXERCISES

THE PRINTER'S PREFACE TO THE READER

I HAD some time since conceived the hope, gentle reader, that the letters of this Author, both public and private, might be entrusted to me to be printed in a single volume. But when I learnt that those who had the sole rights objected, for certain reasons, to the issue of the public letters, I decided to rest content with such part as was permitted and to publish the private letters alone. Finding however that they were some-what too few to form a volume of reasonable size, I decided to treat with the author through a common friend and obtain his sanction to the publication in addition of any small work he might chance to have kept by him, to fill up the space and compensate for the paucity of the letters. This friend prevailed upon him to look through his papers, scattered among which he eventually chanced upon these youthful productions, and yielded to his friend's importunity regarding them. So, finding that they were approved by this common friend, in whose judgment I fully concurred, and that the Author himself was not dissatisfied with them, I had no hesitation in publishing them, youthful work though they are, in the hope that I should find them as saleable (which is my chief personal concern) as those who originally heard them delivered found them enjoyable.

THE PRIVATE LETTERS OF JOHN MILTON, OF ENGLAND, COMPLETE IN ONE VOLUME

1 *To* THOMAS YOUNG, his tutor

ALTHOUGH my intention was, my dearest Master, to send you a letter carefully composed in metrical form, yet I did not feel satisfied without writing another as well, in prose; for that unparalleled and matchless gratitude, which your goodness toward me needs must arouse in my heart, could not find expression in that style of writing which is fast bound and fettered by definite feet and syllables, but only in a style free from all such restrictions, or rather in an Asiatic flow of words, if that might be.

Yet it would be far beyond my power to express fully all that I owe to you, even were I to drain dry all the springs of eloquence and exhaust all the commonplaces of rhetoric which Aristotle and the famous logician of Paris together have amassed.

You complain, as well you may, that the letters you have received from me are far too scarce and too short. I for my part feel less remorse at having been found wanting in so pleasant and attractive a duty, than joy or even exultation at finding that the place I hold in your esteem is such as to demand frequent letters from me. As for my never having written to you for more than three years, I beg you not to think the worst of this, but graciously to put a kindly interpretation upon it, in accordance with your own wonderful gentleness and fair-mindedness. For, upon my oath, I honour you as a father, have ever regarded you with the deepest reverence, and have only feared to cause you annoyance by my importunity in writing. I have indeed done my utmost to ensure that if nothing else commended my letters to you, their rarity at least should do so.

Furthermore, the intense longing which I feel for you leads me constantly to fancy that you are indeed present and that I speak to you and see you face to face, and to assuage my griefs, as men in love often do, by the vain illusion of your presence. Hence I fear, once I set about writing to you, that I may suddenly be forced to realise how many miles separate you from me, and so my grief at your absence, now almost stilled, may start into renewed life and shatter my soothing dreams.

I received some time ago your most welcome gift of a Hebrew Bible.

I write this in London, among the distractions of the town, not, as usual, surrounded by books. So if anything in this letter fails to please you or to fulfil your expectations, it shall be made good in another, upon which more pains have been bestowed, as soon as I return to the haunts of the Muses.

London, March 26th, 1625

2   *To* ALEXANDER GILL

I HAVE received your letter, and also the verses, which gave me intense delight. They are indeed magnificent, inspired throughout by a truly poetic majesty and a spirit worthy of Virgil himself. I knew well enough how impossible it would prove for one gifted with your genius to renounce Poetry and banish from his inmost heart that heaven-sent inspiration and that sacred and celestial fire. For of you one may truly say, as Claudian said of himself, "Phoebus alone is my life's breath". And so, if you have broken the promise you made to yourself, I have nothing but praise for your fickleness, as you call it, in this respect, and for your dishonourable conduct, if such it is. And I am as proud of being chosen by you to give an opinion upon so noble a poem, and feel as greatly honoured, as if the gods of music themselves had asked my judgment on a contest between them—an experience which, they say, once befell Tmolus, the local god of the Lydian mountain. Indeed I know not whether to congratulate Henry of Nassau more upon the capture of the city or upon your verses, for I do not believe that this victory has brought in its train anything more noble or more worthy of renown than this poem of yours.

Now that we hear you sound such triumphant and sonorous trumpet-tones in honour of our allies' success, what a laureate we shall look to find in you, if at last our own fortunes should mend and claim your congratulatory Muse!

Farewell then, my accomplished friend, and accept my most heartfelt thanks for your verses.

London, May 20th, 1628

3 *To* THE SAME

IN my last letter I did not so much answer yours, as excuse myself from answering, and so tacitly promise to write another letter soon, to reply rather more fully to your friendly challenge. But even apart from this promise, I must admit that you have every right to claim a letter, for I consider that every letter of yours demands two of mine in return; or rather, to be more accurate, it cannot be requited even by a hundred.

As to the composition of which I wrote with some obscurity, I enclose it herewith. When your letter arrived, I was very short of time, and had just begun to work on it at high pressure. For a certain Fellow of our College, who was to take part in a philosophical disputation at the last Commencement, being himself already long past such frivolous trifles and occupied with serious business, entrusted to my youthful efforts the verses which have to be composed for the disputation in accordance with the annual custom. These have been committed to print, and I have sent them to you, knowing you to be a most acute judge of poetry in general and a most fair one of mine in particular. If you will be so kind as to send me yours in return, you will certainly not find anyone to whom they would give greater pleasure, though you might, I confess, find one more fitted to do them justice.

Whenever I call to mind your almost constant conversations with me, the like of which I vainly seek even in the very seat of learning, the University itself, I realise at once, to my sorrow, of how much profit my absence deprives me. For I never quitted your company without some clear increase or *crescendo* of learning, just as if I had paid a visit to some mart of erudition. At any rate, so far as I know, there are but one or two among us who do not take their flight to theology before ever they are fledged, almost untrained and uninitiated in literature and philosophy alike. And even of theology they are content with a mere smattering, if it be but enough to enable them to piece together after a fashion some little homily and patch it up as it were out of scraps of other men's rags. So much so, that there is a serious risk of our clergy gradually falling into the popish ignorance of former ages.

As for myself, since I find here hardly any congenial fellow-students, I should turn my eyes straightway back to London, if I were not planning this Long Vacation to bury myself deep in literary retirement, and so to speak take cover in the precincts of the Muses. As this is your regular habit, I feel it to be little less than impious to trouble your peace any longer at present. And so farewell.

Cambridge, July 2nd, 1628

4 *To* THOMAS YOUNG

ON reading your letter, my dearest Master, only one thing seemed to me superfluous, namely your apology for delay in writing. Although nothing could possibly be more welcome to me than your letters, how could or ought I to hope that you would be so little occupied with serious and sacred duties as always to be able to spare time to reply to me?—especially as that is purely a favour on your part, and not in any way an obligation. Moreover, any suspicion of your having forgotten me is absolutely impossible after all the kindnesses you have shown me of late. For I do not see why you should consign to oblivion one upon whom you have showered so many favours.

I gladly accept the invitation to your country home as soon as spring has well set in, to enjoy the delights of the season, and no less of your conversation, and I will retire for a while from the noise of town to your Stoa in the land of the Iceni, as if it were the famous Portico of Zeno or Cicero's Tuscan villa. There, in a kingly spirit though with modest means, like some Regulus or Curius, you reign peacefully over your little estate, and, despising fortune, triumph over wealth, ambition, pomp, luxury, and all that common men admire and gape at.

For the rest, you who ask pardon for tardiness will I hope in your turn grant pardon for my hastiness: for as I had put off this letter to the last moment, I chose rather to send a short and somewhat unpolished letter than not to write at all.

Farewell, my honoured friend.

Cambridge, July 21*st,* 1628

5 *To* ALEXANDER GILL

IF you had made me a present of gold, or of richly chased vessels, or of anything of that sort which men admire, I should certainly be ashamed not to recompense you in my turn so far as lay within my power. By giving me, the day before yesterday, such a brilliant and charming poem in hendecasyllabics, you have made me the more anxious, as its value is beyond that of gold, to find some precious object with which to requite so delightful a gift. I had indeed a few compositions of my own in that style at hand, but thought none of them worthy to be sent in emulation of your own gift. I therefore send what is not entirely my own, but partly the work of that truly divine poet, this Ode of whom I set about translating into Greek heroic metre at daybreak one day last week, before I was up, not of any set purpose, but on some sudden impulse. I hoped thus to have something not unworthy to rank beside your work, relying on the help of one who surpasses you in his subject as much as you do me in skill. If there is anything in it which fails to come up to the standard you usually expect of my work, I must tell you that this is the first and only Greek verse I have composed since I left your school; my preference being, as you know, for Latin or English. The fact is, that anyone who spends time or trouble on Greek verse nowadays is apt to run the risk of piping to deaf ears.

Farewell, and expect me (God willing) at the booksellers' in London on Monday. Meanwhile, if you can do anything to further my cause with the Doctor, this year's President of the College, through your friendship with him, I beg of you to go to him as soon as may be, for my sake.

Again, farewell.

Dated from our suburban house, December 4th, 1634

6 *To* CHARLES DIODATI

AT last I see what you are driving at—to get the better of me by obstinate silence. If so, very well, enjoy your little triumph; I am the first to write, as you see. All the same, if ever the question arises between us why neither has written to the other for so long, you may well find that I have far the better excuse. For I am by nature backward and slow to write, as you well know, while you, on the contrary, are always ready, either by nature or by habit, to engage in epistolary conversation of this kind. This too is on my side, that your method of study is, as I know, such as to allow of frequent breathing-spaces, visits to friends, a good deal of writing and not infrequent journeys; while my own disposition is such that no delay, no rest, no thought or care for anything else, can divert me from my purpose, until I reach my goal and complete some great cycle of my studies. This is the one and only reason, I beg you to believe, why I am reluctant to enter into any voluntary engagements; but I am not so dilatory in replying to favours received, my good Diodati; and I have never failed to repay any letter of yours by one of mine when it was due.

What am I to say of your having written to your bookseller, and frequently to your brother, as I hear? Either of these, as they live so near, would readily have undertaken to forward letters to me, had there been any.

But my chief complaint is that you broke the promise you made to pay me a visit on leaving town. If you had even once thought of your failure to carry out this promise you would have had an excellent reason for writing.

These are grounds enough, I think, for a formal accusation against you; the defence is your affair.

But meanwhile, what is the cause of your silence? Are you in good health? Are there any budding scholars in your part of the world whose society and talk you can enjoy as we used to do each other's? When do you return? How long do you intend to stay among those Eskimos? Please answer each one of my questions; but be sure that the interest I take in your affairs is nothing new, for you must know that early in the autumn, when I was on a journey, I went out of my way to see your brother, on purpose to find out how you were. Besides, not long ago, happening to hear in London from someone or other that you were in town, I rushed off post-haste, and, as I might say, *ventre à terre*, to your lodgings; but it was all "the dream of a shade", for you were nowhere to be found. Therefore, if you can conveniently do so, come quickly, and settle in some place which may at least give better hope of our being able to pay occasional visits to each other: I only wish you could be as near a neighbour to us in the country as you are in town—but be that as God wills.

I have much more to say to you about myself and about my studies, but would rather tell you by word of mouth; and to-morrow I am due to return to my country home, and I am on the point of starting for the journey, so that I have barely time to scribble this note to you. Farewell.

London, September 2nd, 1637

7 *To* THE SAME

AT last I perceive the reason for your frequent repetition of good wishes for my health, which others are as a rule content to express but once in their letters: you would give me to understand that in addition to mere wishes, which were all that you yourself could formerly give, and all that others can give even now, you can now add the crowning gift of your skill and of the whole might of Medicine. For you wish me good health a thousandfold, to my heart's content, to the utmost of my capacity, or even more. Why, you must just have been created High Steward of Health, to judge by the way you make free with Health's store-cupboard; or else Health herself must have become your poor dependent, so magnificently do you play the wealthy patron and command her obedience. So pray accept my congratulations and thanks, which are doubly due to you, first for your friendly interest and secondly for the notable skill you have acquired.

I waited long for a letter from you, according to our agreement; but in spite of having received none up to the present, I have not on that account, believe me, allowed my old good-will toward you to cool in the least; for I felt sure that you would put forward the same plea in defence of your dilatoriness as you did at the beginning of our correspondence, one which you have every right to make use of, and which the friendly relations between us fully justify. For I would not have true friendship tried by the test of letters and good wishes, which may all be feigned; but its roots and the source of its strength should go deep into the mind, and it should spring from a pure origin, so that, even were all tokens of mutual regard to cease, yet it should endure throughout life, untainted by suspicion or recrimination. For its nurture the written word is less essential than a lively recollection of virtues on both sides. Nor does it follow that, in default of your writing, there is nothing to supply the omission; your integrity writes to me in your stead, and indites true letters on the tablets of my heart; the purity of your life and your love of virtue write to me, your whole character too, far above the common, writes to me and commends you to me more and more.

So, now that you have entered the despotic strong-hold of Medicine, pray do not terrify me with your threats or reckon up the account in detail and demand of me the repayment in full of all those thousand good healths, should ever I prove a traitor to friendship, which God forbid. But remove that formidable embargo which you have put upon my freedom, forbidding me to be sick without your kind permission. To avert your threats, I assure you that it is impossible for me not to love such men as yourself, for though I know not God's intent toward me in other respects, yet of this I am sure, that he has imbued me especially with a mighty passion for Beauty. Ceres never sought her daughter Proserpine (as the legend tells) with greater ardour than I do this Idea of Beauty, like some image of loveliness; ever pursuing it, by day and by night, in every shape and form ("for many forms there are of things divine") and following close in its footprints as it leads. And so, whensoever I find one who spurns the base opinions of common men, and dares to be, in thought and word and deed, that which the wisest minds throughout the ages have approved; whensoever, I say, I find such a man, to him I find myself impelled forthwith to cleave. And if I am fated, either by nature or destiny, never to attain this high honour and glory in my own proper person, for all my toil and striving, yet sure I am that neither god nor man shall forbid me to honour and revere all my days those who have won such glory as this, or are happily striving toward it.

To change the subject, I know it is time to satisfy your curiosity. You make many eager enquiries, even asking about my thoughts. I will tell you, Diodati, but let me whisper it in your ear, to spare my blushes, and allow me for a moment to speak to you in a boastful strain. What am I thinking about? you ask. So help me God, of immortality. What am I doing? Growing wings and learning to fly; but my Pegasus can only rise on tender pinions as yet, so let my new wisdom be humble.

To be serious, my plan is to take rooms in one of the Inns of Court, where I hope to find a pleasant and shady spot in which to stroll, and which may afford a more convenient dwelling-place, among congenial compan-

14

ions, when I wish to stay at home, and a more suitable *point d'appui* if I prefer to roam abroad; here my life is, as you know, obscure and cramped.

Of my studies too I will tell you. My study of Greek history has brought me, by steady work, to the point at which they ceased to be Greeks. I have spent much time on the obscure history of Italy under the Lombards, Franks, and Germans, down to the time when it was set free by Rudolf, King of Germany. What follows, the history of each independent state, will be best studied separately.

But what are you doing? How long will you continue to be engrossed in domestic affairs, like a dutiful son, forgetful of your friends in town? Unless this stepmotherly warfare is worse than that against the Dacians or Sarmatians, you must certainly make haste, and take up your winter quarters, at any rate, with us. Meanwhile, if it is not troubling you too much, please send me Giustiniani's History of Venice; I promise either to keep it safe till you come, or if you prefer, to return it to you in a short time. Farewell.

London, September 23rd, 1637

8 *To* BENEDETTO BUONMATTEI of Florence

IN preparing a new grammar of your native language, Benedetto Buonmattei, to which your are even now putting the finishing touches, you are entering upon a path to fame already trodden by some men of the highest eminence. At the same time it is evident that you are rousing in the breasts of your countrymen the hope and expectation that your own labours will illumine, amplify, or at any rate polish and re-arrange the work of your predecessors. If your countrymen do not themselves perceive that they are under no common obligation to you for this they must indeed be ungrateful.

15

The first place and highest honour are, it is true, due to the man who has the ability to mould the character of his people wisely and to rule them in peace and war by the most enlightened ordinances. But second only to him I would place the man who devotes his powers to establishing by rules and precepts the idiom and usage of the language, whether written or spoken, accepted as correct in the best period, and who circumscribes it about by a barrier which must never be passed, under penalties almost as severe as those laid down by Romulus himself. To compare the benefits conferred by these two—it is the former alone who has the power of making the social life of the people just and pure, but the latter alone who can make it humane, rich, and refined, which are the qualities next to be desired. The former supplies a noble patriotism and courageous counsels in face of a hostile invasion; but the latter undertakes the task of repressing and crushing, by means of a magistracy of cultured taste and a police of good authors, that barbarism which constantly besets men's minds and which is the most subtle and insidious foe to their characters. For we ought not to minimise the importance of the purity or corruption of the language, and of the degree of correctness with which it is commonly used. This indeed more than once played a part in the welfare of Athens. It is Plato's opinion that an alteration in the style and fashion of dress portends grave disorders and changes in the State; I would maintain rather that when the language falls into corruption and decay the downfall of the State and a period of degradation and obscurity are at hand. For is not the use of words which are illiterate and mean, incorrect in form, or wrongly pronounced, a very clear indication of a slothful and sluggish disposition among the people, and a proneness to submit to any form of slavery? On the other hand, we have never heard of an empire or a country which did not enjoy at least moderate prosperity as long as its people continued to cultivate and take a proper pride in their language. Consider then, Benedetto, what deep and lasting gratitude you will assuredly win from your fellow-countrymen, if you do but persevere in rendering this service to your country. This I say, not in the expectation that any of these points have escaped you, but in the belief that your thoughts are much more set on the services you can render to your country than on the gratitude which your country ought most properly to pay to you.

I will now proceed to point out the rare opportunity of being of service to foreigners which now offers, if you care to take it. Among them there is no one with any pretensions to superior intellect or to culture and elegance but counts the Tuscan language among his chief delights, and even considers it an essential part of his serious studies; especially if he has drunk either nothing or but a small draught of Greek and Latin. For my own part, I have not merely sipped of both these languages, but have drunk as deeply of them as any man of my years; yet I can often partake with eagerness and delight of the feast afforded by the great Dante, by Petrarch, and by many another of your writers. Not Attic Athens herself, with her clear stream of Ilissus, nor ancient Rome, beside the Tiber, have had the power to make me lose my affection for your Arno and the hills of Fiesole, or cease to visit them with joy.

Consider now, I beg, whether there is not something providential in my having been sent to spend these few days among you, your latest guest from foreign lands—one than whom your country has, I think, no more devoted admirer. For this reason it behoves you to remember what I have so often urged upon you; namely that you would consent to add to your work, already begun and in part completed, a short chapter on the correct pronunciation of the language, treated as simply as the subject will permit, and so earn the gratitude of us foreigners. For up to the present the authorities on your language seem entirely to have forgotten us, and to have thought only of giving satisfaction to their own countrymen. Yet, in my opinion, they would have acted in the better interests both of their own fame and of the reputation of the Italian tongue if they had so set forth their teaching as if men of every race might reasonably be expected to desire a knowledge of that language. So far as their work went, they gave the impression that you Italians did not care to spread your knowledge beyond the confines of the Alps.

Therefore the glory of this achievement has not been tasted by any other, and is reserved for you fresh and pure to this day. There will be yet another claim to fame no less your own, if you will go to the trouble of indicating severally who among all the host of authors can justly claim the second place after the acknowledged masters of the Florentine tongue, who excels in tragedy, who writes lively and elegant comedy, who shows acuteness or depth of thought in letters or dialogues, and who has a noble style in historical writing. With this guide, a student who so desires will not find it difficult to select the best, and will at the same time have a sound foothold if he wishes to go further afield. In this attempt you will have as your models Cicero and Fabius among the ancients, but none, so far as I know, among your own contemporaries.

I believe, if I am not mistaken, that whenever we have chanced to speak of this, your courtesy and kindliness have led you to accede to my request; but I do not desire to evade the obligation of entreating this favour in due form and set phrase. For while your own virtue and modesty claim but the lowest place and the least regard for your work, I am anxious that its own worth and the respect I myself feel should proclaim its just and true value. And indeed it is but fitting that we should not fail to pay the honour due to a benefactor in proportion to the graciousness with which he has bestowed his favours upon us.

For the rest, should you ask why, on this occasion, I

have made use of Latin rather than of your own tongue, my object was to confess freely, by writing in Latin, my imperfect knowledge and grasp of that language in which I crave your guidance and instruction. I hoped by this means to prevail with you the more readily, and believed that if I brought with me from Latium that hoary and venerable mother to plead her daughter's cause with me, you would not find it in your heart to deny any request supported by her authority, her sanctity, and her majesty, revered from time immemorial. Farewell.

Florence, September 10th, 1638

9 *To* LUCAS HOLSTENIUS, at the Vatican in Rome

ALTHOUGH I can, and often do, remember the great courtesy and friendliness which I have received during my passage through Italy, yet there is perhaps no one from whom I could properly say that I have received greater proofs of goodwill than yourself, on so short an acquaintance. For when I went to visit you at the Vatican you received me with the utmost cordiality although I was completely unknown to you, except for anything which Cherubini may have told you previously. You afterwards were so good as to admit me to the Library, where I had the opportunity of seeing the rich collection of volumes and the large number of Greek manuscripts as well, enriched by your annotations. Some of these have never been seen in our time, but lie waiting, like the souls in Virgil "enclosed within the confines of a green vale, waiting to take their journey to the world above", and seemed to demand the helping hand and obstetric skill of the printer; others have already been published by you, and have been eagerly received by scholars throughout the world. You presented me, moreover, with two copies of one of these as a parting gift.

19   2-2

In addition to all this, I cannot but think that it was owing to your recommending me to his Eminence Cardinal Francesco Barberini that at the public concert which he gave a few days later with truly Roman magnificence, he himself stood at the door to receive me, sought me out in that great crowd, and almost taking me by the hand pressed me to enter, with every mark of honour. When I went next day to pay my respects as his graciousness demanded, it was again you whom I had to thank for procuring me an audience and the opportunity of conversing with him. The great man, who, for all his high rank, is the soul of courtesy and kindliness, granted me an audience which, considering the time and place, inclined to lengthiness rather than brevity.

I do not indeed know, my learned friend Holstenius, whether you have singled me out for such remarkably friendly and hospitable treatment, or whether you make a practice of bestowing similar favours on all Englishmen, on account of your three years' residence at the University of Oxford. If the latter is the case, you have chosen a generous way of repaying your debt to England, and one which reflects honour upon yourself, and you merit equal gratitude from each one of us in particular and from our country in general. But if the former is the case, and you have singled me out above all others and held me worthy to be honoured with your friendship, I congratulate myself on your choice, while attributing the honour to your kindness rather than to my own deserts.

As to the commission which you seemed to entrust to me, of inspecting the Codex Mediceus, I was forward in laying it before my friends, but they give very little hope of its being executed at present. They tell me it is a rule of that library that unless one has previously obtained permission nothing may be copied, and that one is not allowed even to make notes. They say, however, that there is one Giovanni Battista Doni at Rome, who has been appointed public lecturer in Greek at Florence, and is shortly expected. It would be easy to obtain what you desire through him, though I should have been very glad if I could have been of some better service in forwarding an object so desirable, since in so honourable and excellent an undertaking you have the right to command the help of all men everywhere and to expect every possible assistance and facility.

For the rest, you will lay me under a fresh obligation if you will convey my most profound respects to his Eminence the Cardinal. I have constantly in mind his great virtues, his zeal for truth, so nobly shown in his encouragement of the liberal arts, and even more his gentle and, so to say, lowly loftiness of spirit, which alone knows how to rise by its own submissiveness. One may indeed say of it, as Callimachus said of Ceres, though with a different meaning, "her steps were set upon the earth, but her head reached unto Olympus". His conduct may serve to show other princes what a vast difference there is between the forbidding haughtiness and lordly arrogance which they affect, and true magnanimity. So long as he is alive, no one, I believe, could any longer feel the loss of the Este, Farnese, or Medici families, who were once the patrons of the learned.

Farewell then, my learned friend Holstenius, and wherever I may be in future, count me, I beg you, among those who are most devotedly attached to you and to your interests, if you hold me worthy of the honour.

Florence, March 30th, 1639

10 *To* CARLO DATI, nobleman, of Florence

SINCE I am unable to express as well as the case demands, my dear Carlo, the great and fresh delight which your unexpected letter brought me, I will try to give you at any rate some idea of it by speaking of the sorrow, which is the almost invariable accompaniment of all human joy. While glancing over the first part of your letter, in which there is so charming a rivalry of elegance and friendship, I could have declared that it gave me pure joy, especially as I perceived that you meant to secure the victory to friendship. But as soon as I came to the passage in which you say that you had already written me three letters, which must, I know, have been lost, then the pure joy I had hitherto felt began to be clouded and troubled by sad regrets. Soon an even more depressing thought came into my mind, a thought which often makes me lament my fortune, namely that those who are closely bound to me by the fact of neighbourhood or by some other tie of no real importance, either by chance or by some legal claim, though they have nothing else to commend them to me, are with me every day, deafen me with their noise, and, I swear, torment me as often as they choose; while those who are so greatly endeared to me by sympathy of manners, disposition and tastes, are almost all separated from me either by death or by the cruel accident of distance, and are as a rule snatched from my sight so swiftly that I am compelled to spend my life in almost perpetual loneliness. It gives me great satisfaction to hear that since I left Florence you have always been anxious about my health and have never forgotten me, and to find that the feelings which I had, perhaps perversely, imagined to be mine alone, were in fact fully reciprocated. I can assure you that my departure gave real pain to myself as well, and that it left a sting which I still feel acutely whenever I recollect all the kind and congenial friends and companions I left behind me in that one city, so distant but so well beloved. It was with the utmost reluctance that I tore myself away. I appeal to the tomb of Damon, which I shall ever hallow and revere. When, in composing my elegy on his death, I was overcome by sadness and grief and sought what solace I might, and some short respite from sorrow, I could find no greater source of joy than the happy recollection of all my friends in Florence, and of yourself in particular. This you must already have discovered for yourself in reading the poem, which, as I now first learn, did not fail to reach you. I had indeed taken particular care to send it, that you might find a very slight proof of my ability, but a very strong one of my affection for you, if only in those few personal verses which form a kind of decorative insertion. I hoped by this means to induce either you or someone else to write to me; feeling that if I were the first to write I should be under the necessity either of writing to all, or else, by showing a preference to one rather than another, incurring the resentment of the rest, should they discover it; for I hoped that I had still many friends in Italy who had a strong claim to my letters. As it is, you are the first of all to write, and by the friendly challenge of your letter and by writing three times in succession you have made it incumbent upon me to fulfil the duty of replying to you, which I have long owed, and so released me from the fear of giving offence to others.

I confess, however, that there have been other reasons for my silence, in the grave disturbances which have troubled England since my return: these almost immediately compelled me to turn my attention from the pursuit of learning to the preservation of my life and fortunes as best might be. You can imagine that any peace and quiet for the leisurely pursuit of literature was out of the question in the midst of civil war, bloodshed, flight, and rapine. Still (since you enquire about my work), even in this time of tribulation, I have been able to publish a fair amount in my native English; if it were not in this language I should gladly send it to you, since I have the highest esteem for your opinion. I will shortly send any of my poems that are in Latin, since you ask me. I should indeed have done so long since of my own accord but for this: I was afraid that the rather harsh expressions about the Pope which are to be found in a few pages might offend your ears. As it is, I beg you to persuade my other friends (for of your own indulgence I feel secure) to extend to me, whenever I have to speak of your religion in the way which is customary among us, the same indulgence which you were all in the habit of granting, not merely to your own Dante and Petrarch on similar occasions, but, with remarkable tolerance, to the freedom of speech which you used to allow me when I was with you.

I read your description of King Louis' funeral with enjoyment. In it I recognise the inspiration of Mercury —not however the Mercury of the cross-roads and the market, to whose service you playfully declare yourself to be devoted of late, but the Mercury who is the friend of the Muses and the patron of men of a mercurial temperament.

It remains for us to find some way or means by which in future our letters may go and come in safety. This should not be very difficult, since many of our merchants have considerable business with you, and their agents travel to and fro every week, while their ships set sail in either direction almost as often. I will entrust these arrangements to the bookseller James, or to my good friend his master, I hope with safety.

Meanwhile, my dear Carlo, I send my good wishes to you, and to Coltellini, Francini, Frescobaldi, Malatesti, the younger Chimentelli, and to any other of my good friends whom you know; and pray convey my respects to the whole of Gaddi's Academy. Meanwhile, farewell.

London, April 21*st,* 1647

24

11 *To* HERMANN MYLIUS, Agent for the COUNT OF OLDENBURG

BEFORE replying to your letter of December 17th to me, my noble friend Hermann, I must first explain to you why I did not answer before, lest perchance you should condemn me for my long silence. First, then, I must tell you that the delay was due to that constant enemy of mine, poor health; secondly, to a sudden and unavoidable removal to another house, which was necessary for my health, and which, as it happened, I had begun on the very day on which your letter reached me; and finally to a feeling of shame that I had no information to send you about your affairs which could give you satisfaction. For the next day I chanced to meet Mr Frost and enquired particularly of him whether any decision had been reached about a reply to you (for I myself was often absent from the Council on account of my health). He replied, with some concern, that nothing was as yet decided, and that he was unable to do anything to expedite the matter. I therefore thought it better to say nothing for the time being, rather than to write off at once what I knew would vex you, in the hope that I should later have the pleasure of being able to send you news in accord with my own wishes and your urgent desire. And this I have to-day, I hope, accomplished. For after I had once or twice reminded the President of your affairs, at a meeting of the Council, he brought the question forward at once, and a discussion was fixed for the following day to decide on an immediate reply to you.

In being the first to give you this news, as I was anxious to be, I hope that it will give you satisfaction and at the same time afford some small proof of my anxiety to serve you.

Westminster

12 *To* the renowned LEONARD PHILARAS, of Athens, Ambassador of the DUKE OF PARMA to the KING OF FRANCE

I HAD already heard of your goodwill toward me, most accomplished Philaras, and also of your favourable judgment of my *Defence of the English People*. This I learnt from a reference in your letter to Monsieur Augier, a man whose signal services in transacting the diplomatic business of our Republic have earned him high esteem. Now I have received through him likewise your kind message, together with your portrait and the eulogy which your virtues so well deserve, and finally your most courteous letter.

Though I have no small regard for the abilities of the Germans, and even of the Danes and the Swedes, yet I cannot but set the highest value on the opinion of me formed by you, a native of Athens, the capital of Attica, and one who, after successfully completing your studies in Italy, have won the highest honour for your great experience in practical affairs. For since Alexander the Great, while waging war at the ends of the earth, confessed that he had endured all those hardships of war "for the sake of the glory he would win in the eyes of the Athenians", why should not I think it a matter for congratulation and a high honour, to be praised by a man in whose person the talents of the ancient Athenians and their far-famed virtues seem to be reborn after so long a lapse of time and to flourish once more. I gladly confess that it is above all by studying constantly, from my youth up, the works of the many able men who have sprung from Athens that I have acquired whatever literary skill I may have.

If I possessed by gift or inheritance from them such powers of persuasion as would enable me to send out our fleet and army to free Greece, the home of eloquence, from the Ottoman tyrant (such is the noble enterprise

26

in which you seem to implore my aid), I would assuredly do so, for it is the object of all others nearest to
my heart and mind. For what aim did even the bravest
and most eloquent of the ancients set before themselves
as more glorious or more worthy of their talents than
"to procure the freedom and independence of Greece"
by force of words or by acts of courage? But there is
also another object for which we should strive, and one
which is, in my opinion, the most important of all
objects, namely to revive and re-awaken in the hearts of
the Greeks the courage, industry, and endurance which
they once possessed, by recounting their ancient virtues.
If this can but be accomplished, as we may expect it to
be by none better than by you, uniting as you do the
qualities of burning patriotism, practical wisdom, and
military skill, with a high passion for regaining your
country's ancient liberty—then, I am confident, the
Greeks will not be wanting to themselves, nor will any
other nation be wanting to the Greeks. Farewell.

London, June 1652

13 *To* RICHARD HEATH

A NY help I have ever been able to give, my worthy
friend, in advancing your studies or in grounding
them well, amounts to nothing or at any rate to
very little. But I am delighted, for more reasons than
one, that such as it is it should have been bestowed on a
nature of such promise, though only tardily recognised
as such, and with results so excellent and so happy. I
rejoice, too, that it has borne such good fruit in providing the Church with a virtuous pastor, the State with
a good citizen, and myself with a very dear friend. Of
this I find clear evidence in the whole tenor of your life
and in the soundness of your religious and political
views, and especially in the remarkable loyalty of your

nature, which neither absence nor lapse of time can quench or diminish. For you could not feel so much gratitude to all who have been of even the least assistance to you in your progress if you had not made a more than ordinary advance in virtue and piety and in the study of all that is noblest. Therefore, my dear pupil (as I should wish to call you, if I may), be assured that I count you among my dearest friends, and that nothing would give me greater happiness than that, your convenience and circumstances permitting, you should take up your residence in this neighbourhood, thus enabling us to share each other's life and studies more frequently and with greater pleasure, as indeed I perceive to be your desire also. But be that as God wills and as may be most expedient for you.

You may, if you wish, write any further letters in English (though you have in fact attained considerable proficiency in Latin), to avoid the possibility that the labour of composition should make either of us less ready to write, and to enable the sympathy between us to be more freely expressed, unhindered by the shackles of a foreign tongue.

You can, I think, confidently entrust your letters to any of the servants of the family you mention. Farewell.

Westminster, December 13th, 1652

14 *To* HENRY OLDENBURG, Agent for Bremen to the English Parliament

YOUR former letter, honoured Sir, was delivered to me just as your messenger, I was told, was on the point of returning; there was consequently no possibility of replying then. I had intended to do so at the earliest opportunity, but some unexpected business prevented me. If this had not been the case, I should certainly not have sent the book to you in so unpro-

tected a condition, without any excuse—although, it is
true, it has its title of "Defence" to protect it. And now
I have your second letter, in which your thanks are out
of all proportion to the slightness of the gift.

I have more than once thought of replying to your
Latin letters in English, to give you every possible opportunity of writing as well as of speaking English, as
I have no doubt you can with equal accuracy. You have
indeed learnt to speak our language more accurately
and fluently than any other foreigner I have ever
known. But I will leave it to you to do as pleases you
best.

In what you say about the subject-matter, you evidently agree with me in thinking that such a "Cry to
Heaven" is beyond the reach of human senses; so that
the man who so shamelessly claims to have heard it
must be a rank impostor.

You have expressed some doubt as to his identity;
but on previous occasions on which we have discussed
the question, at a time when you had recently returned
from Holland, you never appeared to have any doubt of ·
the author's being Morus; such was indeed, you told
me, the general opinion in that country, nor was any
other name suggested. If you have since acquired any
other information, I beg you to tell me of it.

As to my handling of the subject-matter, I sincerely
wish, as I readily admit, that I did not disagree with
you; but in daring to do so to some extent, what could
give me greater encouragement than the sound judgment of prudent men like yourself, and their approval,
which is untainted by any trace of flattery. It would not
be difficult to persuade me to engage in other under-
takings, though I doubt whether they would be nobler
or more useful (for what human activity could be
nobler or more useful than the vindication of liberty?),
if only my health and the loss of my sight (which is a
greater affliction than old age itself), and most of all if
the "cries" of such impostors as this will allow me to do

so. For mere idleness, on the one hand, has never had any charm for me, and on the other, it was much against my will that I found myself obliged to take part in this unexpected contest with the enemies of liberty, at a time when I was engrossed in far different and more delightful occupations. At the same time I do not regret my action, since it was necessary, and I am far from thinking that I have wasted my time to no purpose, as you seem to suggest.

Of this more later. Meanwhile, my learned Sir, I will not take up more of your valuable time, so farewell, and I pray you to count me among your good friends.

Westminster, July 6th, 1654

15 *To* LEONARD PHILARAS, of Athens

FROM my boyhood I have ever been among the most devoted admirers of all that is Greek, and of your own Athens in especial, and I have always had a strong conviction that some day that city would present me with some signal reward for my devotion to her. Nor has the ancient genius of your noble country failed to justify my expectation, by bestowing upon me in you a brother and affectionate friend, born in the city of Athens. For though you knew me only by my writings and were far removed from me in place, you most kindly sought my acquaintance by letter. Later, finding yourself unexpectedly in London, you came to see me, though I could not see you, and have continued to show the same goodwill toward me even though I am afflicted with a misfortune on account of which, it may be, few care to look upon, though many look down upon me. You urge me not to abandon all hope of regaining my sight, and tell me that you have a friend and relative in Paris, Dr Thévenot by name, who is an eminent oculist, and that you intend to consult him about my

30

eyes if I give you the information necessary to enable him to judge of the symptoms and cause of the disease. I will therefore do as you say, that I may not seem to refuse any help which Providence may send me, from whatever quarter it comes.

It is, I suppose, about ten years since I first noticed that my sight was growing weak and dull, and at the same time I began to suffer in the spleen and bowels and to be troubled with flatulence; and in the morning, if I began to read, as was my usual custom, I felt sharp pains in my eyes, and was quite unable to go on; but if I took a little physical exercise my eyes felt better. In looking at a lamp, I saw it surrounded by a kind of rainbow. A little later, a mist formed on the left side of my left eye (that eye became clouded a few years before the other), and prevented me from seeing anything on that side. And objects in front of me seemed smaller if I closed my right eye. In the course of some three years the other eye slowly and gradually failed, and some months before blindness became total everything at which I looked while standing still myself seemed to float about to one side or the other. My forehead and temples seem to be the seat of chronic vapours, which constantly oppress and weigh down my eyes with a sort of sleepy heaviness, especially from dinner-time till evening, so that I am often reminded of the description, in the *Argonautica*, of Phineus, the seer of Salmydessus —"And a dark stupor covered him, and it seemed that the earth reeled round beneath his feet, and he lay in a strengthless trance, speechless".

I must not omit to mention that, before I had quite lost my sight, on first going to bed and lying on one side or the other, I saw a flood of light flashing before my closed eyes; later, as my sight rapidly failed, colours, proportionately less brilliant, seemed to burst from within, with a kind of rush and roar; but now, as if all light were quenched, blackness, or blackness relieved and interwoven with an ashy grey, constantly envelopes me. Yet the mist which is always before my eyes by night as well as by day inclines to white rather than black in colour, and when I move my eyes it seems to admit a faint ray of light as if through a chink.

Even if the doctor is able to see a small spark of hope in this, I am nevertheless prepared and resigned to find my case incurable; and I often reflect that since many days of darkness are destined for every one of us, as the sage warns us, my own darkness has hitherto, by the wondrous grace of God, been rendered much easier to bear than the darkness of death, through the consolation of leisure and study, and the conversation and visits of my friends. And if indeed, as it is written, "Man shall not live by bread alone, but by every word that proceedeth out of the mouth of God", why should not a man find repose in the belief that he does not depend for his sight upon his eyes alone, but upon the guidance and providence of God? Of a surety, while He cares and provides for me, as He does, and takes me by the hand and leads me, surely I will cheerfully grant my eyes dispensation from their task, since so it has seemed good to Him.

Whatever the outcome may be, I now bid you farewell, my dear Philaras, with as much courage and composure as if I had the eyes of Lynceus.

Westminster, September 28th, 1654

16 *To* LEO DE AITZEMA

IT is very gratifying to me to find that your present recollection of me equals the goodwill which formerly you so kindly showed me by paying me several visits when you were in this country.

As to the book on divorce, which you tell me you have entrusted to someone for translation into Dutch, I should myself have preferred that you had it translated into Latin; because I know only too well how the common rout usually receive uncommon opinions, through my experience in the case of these books. For there are *three* tractates of mine on this subject: one, in two books, in which there is a full discussion of the doctrine and discipline of divorce (this is the title of the book); a second, entitled *Tetrachordon*, in which the four chief Scriptural texts bearing on the question are explained; and a third, *Colasterion*, which contains an answer to a certain sciolist. Which of these tractates you are having translated, or in which edition, I do not know. There were two editions of the first, the second edition being much enlarged. If you do not already know of this, or if there is anything else I can do for you, as for instance to send you the corrected edition or the rest of the tractates, I shall be very glad to do my best. For there is no alteration or addition which I would like made to them at present. Therefore, if you carry out your intention, I wish a competent translator for myself, and for you every success in your enterprise.

Westminster, February 5th, 1654/5

17 *To* EZEKIEL SPANHEIM of Geneva

I DO not know how it is that your letters have taken almost three months to reach me, from the date of their despatch. Mine certainly used to reach you much more quickly, for though I have been fully intending to write from one day to the next, I have been prevented by constant business of one kind or another, and now realise that I have incurred a delay of three months more. Please do not infer from my slowness in replying that my gratitude for your kindness to me has grown cold, but rather that the remembrance of it has sunk more deeply into my mind, the longer and more often I have meditated on the duty I owe of repaying it. The tardy discharge of a duty has at least this excuse, that it is more fully admitted when performed so long after than when performed at once.

And first of all you are not at fault in the opinion you express of me in the beginning of your lettter: namely, that it causes me no surprise to be addressed by a foreigner. And you would be perfectly right in supposing that I do not regard any good man as a foreigner or a stranger. I am readily persuaded that such is your character, first because you are the son of so learned and saintly a father, secondly because you enjoy a good reputation among good men, and lastly because you have a hatred of bad men. Since I too happen to be engaged in warfare with these last, Calandrini acted with his usual courtesy and in full accord with my wishes in suggesting to you that it would give me great satisfaction to have your co-operation in the struggle against our common adversary. This you have very kindly afforded me in this same letter, part of which I have taken the liberty (trusting in your regard for me) of inserting as evidence in my defence of myself, though without mentioning the author's name. I will see that the book is sent to you as soon as it is published, if I can find a trustworthy messenger.

Meanwhile I think you can send any letters intended for me without risk under cover to Turretin of Geneva, now staying in London, whose brother at Geneva you know. This letter of mine to you may conveniently be sent through him, and yours to me similarly.

For the rest, be assured that I hold you in the highest esteem, as indeed you deserve, and desire above all your future regard.

Westminster, March 24th, 1654/5

18 *To* the noble youth RICHARD JONES

IONLY received your letter long after you sent it, as
it was mislaid somewhere at your mother's house for
a fortnight or so. I did, however, at last learn from it,
with much satisfaction, of your affection and feelings of
gratitude toward me. Certainly I have always shown
myself worthy both of your excellent mother's good
opinion and confidence, and of your own disposition,
by my affection for you and my faithful admonition.

The place to which you have now retired has, as you
say, a charm of its own and a healthy climate, as well as
a sufficient supply of books for the purposes of university work. If the beauty of its situation were as conducive to the mental profit of those who live in it as it is
to their pleasure, the felicity of that place would be
complete. There is also a well-equipped library; but
unless it enables the students to improve their minds by
the best instruction, it would deserve the name of "book
repository" rather than of "library". You are very well
aware that for this reason the desire to learn and habits
of industry must be added to all these advantages. Take
the utmost care not to forget this and never to give me
occasion to call you to task; and this you will most
readily avoid by paying the strictest heed to the sound
and friendly advice of your friend and associate, the
accomplished Henry Oldenburg.

Farewell, my dearest Richard, and allow me to
exhort and incite you to the practice of virtue and piety,
like a second Timothy, by the example of that excellent
lady your mother.

Westminster

19 *To* HENRY OLDENBURG, Agent for Bremen to the English Parliament

YOUR letter, delivered to me by young Ranelagh, found me rather busy, so that I am obliged to be more brief than I should wish. But you have been as punctilious in carrying out your parting promise of writing as any one could be in discharging a debt on the very day it was due.

Although your retirement is a loss to me, yet, since it gives you pleasure, I congratulate you upon it. I also congratulate you on your happy disposition, which enables you so easily to turn away from both the intrigues and the diversions of town life to the contemplation of higher things. What advantages you find in that retirement other than a good supply of books, I do not know; and I should imagine that the companions you have found there in your studies are students in virtue of their own inclination rather than because of any facilities for study which the place affords—unless, indeed, my acute sense of your absence leads me to be less than just to the place which keeps you from me. Meanwhile you yourself rightly observe that there are too many in that place who confound subjects both human and divine with their own inane subtleties, in order that they may avoid the charge of doing nothing to deserve the high salaries which they receive to the public detriment. But this you understand even better yourself.

The very ancient Chinese chronicles, dating from the time of the Flood, which you tell me the Jesuit Martini has promised, will doubtless be eagerly awaited because of the novelty of the subject; but I do not see what authority or confirmation they can possibly add to the Mosaic books.

Our friend Cyriack, to whom you begged to be remembered, sends his compliments in return. Farewell.

Westminster, June 25th, 1656

20 *To* the noble youth RICHARD JONES

I ATTEMPTED on several occasions to reply to your last letter, but was always prevented by some business or other, such as you know is apt to claim my attention. Later I heard that you had made an excursion into the country near-by. But now your excellent mother will herself deliver this letter to you, on her way to Ireland. Both of us will feel her departure acutely, for to me also she has supplied the place of every family tie.

You are right in feeling assured of my affection for you; and I would have that assurance grow daily firmer, in proportion to the increase in your goodness of disposition and virtue of which you give me proof. This obligation, by God's grace, you not only take upon yourself, but, as if I had exacted a solemn engagement, you bind yourself with full security duly to perform it, promising to submit to judgment and pay the penalty should you fail to carry out your undertaking.

I am delighted with the confidence you have in yourself, which you cannot now go back upon without not merely breaking your promise, but forfeiting your bail as well.

In saying that you like Oxford well enough you do not give me any reason for believing you to have made any progress or grown any wiser; of that you will have to give me very different proofs. You extol the victories of princes and suchlike, in which mere force counts for most, but I would not have you, as the disciple of philosophers, regard such things with too much admiration. For why should one think it so remarkable, if in the country of mutton-heads there are to be found strong horns, able by the violence of their butting to knock down cities and towns? You should, from your youth upward, learn to weigh and discern great characters, not by

37

their brute force and strength, but by their justice and temperance.

Farewell, and give my kindest regards to your companion, the accomplished Henry Oldenburg.

Westminster, September 21*st,* 1656

21   *To* the accomplished youth PETER HEIMBACH

You have abundantly fulfilled, my dear Heimbach, all your promises and every other expectation aroused by your goodness. The only exception is my longing for your return, which you assured me would be within two months at the most. You have now been away nearly three months—unless indeed my desire to have you back makes the time seem longer.

You have amply fulfilled my request about the Atlas. I did not ask you to buy it for me, but only to find out the lowest price of the book. You tell me that this is a hundred and thirty florins; it must, I should think, be the African mountain of that name, and not a book, for which such an outrageous price is asked, as you tell me. The extravagance of printers in the production of books has reached such a pitch, that it now costs as much to furnish a library as a country house. As far as I am concerned, pictures are, on account of my blindness, of little use to me, whose blind eyes wander in vain over the real world, and I am afraid that any money I spent on that book would only seem to make my deprivation more painful to me.

May I ask you to go to this further trouble on my behalf, to find out and inform me on your return of how many volumes the work consists, and which of the two editions, that of Blaeu or that of Jansen, is the more complete and accurate. I hope that your return will be speedy, and that I may receive this information from you in person rather than by another letter.

Meanwhile farewell, and return to us as soon as may be.   *Westminster, November 8th,* 1656

22   *To* the accomplished EMERIC BIGOT

IT gave me great satisfaction, as well it might, that on coming to England you should have singled me out for the honour of a visit. And that you should now again send me greeting by letter, after so long a lapse of time, affords me even greater satisfaction. For you might, in the first instance, have been induced to visit me by what others said, but it is hardly likely that you would renew our acquaintance by writing except by your own desire, or at least your kindness. Hence I have good reason for congratulating myself. For many men have attained a high position by their writings, in whose living voice and daily life there was nothing above the ordinary level or out of the common. If then I can prove my intellect and character to be equal to any writings of mine which may merit approval, I shall at once add weight by my personality to what I have written and derive from my writings an increase of any small personal reputation I may have; since it will be apparent that everything good or praiseworthy which I have written has not been borrowed from authors of established excellence but is entirely original and springs only from the depths of my own mind and heart. Therefore I am glad to find you convinced of my serenity in the great affliction of blindness, and of my friendly interest in foreigners and hospitality to them. I have indeed good reason for patience under the loss of my sight, in hoping that it is not so much lost as retired and withdrawn into myself, and that it serves to sharpen rather than dull the sight of my mind. Thus it is that I feel no resentment against books and have not altogether given up the study of them, great as is the price they have exacted. Against such pettiness I am warned by the example of Telephus, King of the Mysians, who did not refuse to be cured by the very weapon which inflicted the wound.

39

As to the book on the manner of holding Parliaments which is in your possession, I have had the marked passages in it emended, or, if they were doubtful, checked, by the MS. belonging to the illustrious Lord Bradshaw, and by the Cotton MS., as you will see by your note, which I return herewith. In compliance with your desire to know whether an autograph copy of this book exists in the Tower of London, I sent to ask the Keeper of the Records, who is a friend of mine. He replied that no copy of that book exists among those records.

I am most grateful to you for so kindly offering to help me in return to procure literary material. I still need the following Byzantine histories—the *Chronographia* of Theophanes (folio: Greek and Latin), the *Breviarium Historicum* of Constantine Manasses, and the *Excerpta de Antiquitatibus Constantinopolitanis* of Codinus (folio: Greek and Latin), the *Historia et Vitae Romanorum Pontificum* of Anastasius Bibliothecarius (folio). Please add to these, from the same press, if they are yet issued, Michael Glycas and Joannes Sinnamus, whose history follows on that of Anna Comnena. I do not add the request that you should get these as cheaply as possible, partly because there is no need to ask so thrifty a man as yourself to do so, and partly because I hear that the price of these books is fixed and known to all. Mr Stoupe has undertaken to pay you the money in cash, and to see about the most convenient means of transporting the books.

Accept my best wishes for the fulfilment of all your hopes and desires.

Westminster, March 24th, 1656/7

23 *To* the distinguished MR HENRY DE BRASS

I PERCEIVE, Sir, that you very wisely and properly
follow the example of the ancient philosophers in the
conduct of your travels, and aim not merely at the
satisfaction of youthful curiosity, but at the acquisition
of wider knowledge from every possible source. Few
of the young men of to-day who indulge in foreign
travel act in accordance with this principle. And yet,
whenever I consider what you say, I feel that your purpose in visiting foreign lands is not so much to acquire
information from others as to impart it to them, and to
effect an exchange of precious merchandise rather than
to be merely the purchaser of it. I only wish it were as
easy for me to assist and further by every means your
keen desire for learning, as it is pleasing and gratifying
to find my help sought by a man of your outstanding
ability.

You tell me that you have determined to write to me
and ask my advice in the solution of those difficulties
about which historians appear to have been in the dark
for centuries past; but I have certainly never laid claim
to any such power, nor should I dare to do so.

As to your remarks on Sallust, since you insist on my
expressing my opinion, I will freely say that I personally prefer Sallust to every other Latin historian; such
was in fact the almost invariable opinion of the ancients.
Your favourite Tacitus has his merits, the greatest of
which is, in my opinion, that he did his utmost to imitate
Sallust. Through our discussion of this subject, I seem,
so far as I can judge by your letter, to have won you over
to an opinion of that remarkably gifted writer which is
almost identical with my own.

You ask further how, in my judgment, historians can
best attain the end of which Sallust speaks at the opening
of the *Catiline*, when he says that the writing of history
is an extremely difficult art, because of the necessity of

41

adopting a style in harmony with the actions described. My opinion is as follows: one who would be a worthy historian of worthy deeds must possess as noble a spirit and as much practical experience as the hero of the action himself, in order that he may be able to comprehend and measure even the greatest of these actions on equal terms, and, when he has fully grasped them, may be able to set them forth in a pure and chaste style, and in a dignified and impressive manner. I do not demand an ornate style, for it is a historian I am seeking, not a rhetorician. I do not, moreover, approve of the frequent interspersion of general maxims and criticism of events, because in so doing an historian destroys the continuity of the subject and encroaches upon the province of the politician. An historian best fulfils his own proper function by not giving rein to his own fancy and conjectures, when he explains motives and narrates facts, but by following the truth most closely.

I would also mention that special virtue of Sallust, a quality for which he himself particularly extolled Cato, namely that of conciseness. This is a quality which none can possess who does not also possess acute discrimination and a certain restraint. There are many who can offer either elegance of style or an abundance of information; but in combining brevity with fullness, that is to say, in saying much in few words, of all Latin authors Sallust is, in my opinion, easily first.

These are the virtues which I hold it necessary for an historian to possess, if he is to have any hope of writing in a style adequate to the facts he is to relate. But why should I tell you all this? With your intelligence, you are well able to gather as much for yourself; you have indeed already set forth upon a road which, if you follow it steadily, will soon lead you to a point at which you will have no superior to consult; I do most earnestly entreat and urge you so to follow it, with all the authority you allow me to command; for though you do not stand in need of any exhortation, I would not seem to have disappointed your expectations by refusing to reply at all.

Farewell. I wish you every success, as your virtue and your eagerness for knowledge deserve.

Westminster, July 15th, 1657

24 *To* HENRY OLDENBURG

I AM glad to hear that you have arrived safely at Saumur, which is, I believe, your destination. You were right in thinking that I should be particularly glad to hear this, since I have a strong affection for you personally and also know how honourable and praiseworthy is the object of your journey.

But I wish it had been anyone else you please in Charon's boat, rather than yourself in the Charenton boat, who had heard the news which you give me, that so infamous a minister has been called to instruct so illustrious a church; for there is good reason to fear that anyone who expects to reach heaven by the help of so unprincipled a guide will suffer the disappointment of finding himself worlds away from his goal. Woe to that church (may God avert the omen) in which such ministers find favour by tickling men's ears—ministers whom the church, if it would be held truly reformed, would cast out rather than take to itself.

In giving copies of my works only to those who ask for them you act in a proper and seemly way, and in accordance not only with my own wish but also with the view expressed by Horace—"lest in desire to help me you blunder, and bring odium on my book by the officious service of excessive zeal".

A certain learned man, a friend of mine, stayed at Saumur last summer. He wrote to me that there was a demand for the book there. I sent only a single copy. He wrote again to tell me that the book had been enthusiastically received by several men of learning to whom he had shown it. If I had not believed that I should be doing what would please them I should have spared you the trouble and myself the expense. But "if perchance the parcel of my writings prove too heavy and gall your shoulders, fling it away at once, rather than dash down in ill temper the pack-saddle when you reach your destination".

I presented your compliments to Lawrence as you requested. For the rest, I beg you to make it your first aim and object to maintain your own and your pupil's good health and to return to us as soon as may be when you have accomplished your purpose.

Westminster, August 1st, 1657

25 *To* the noble youth RICHARD JONES

I AM delighted to hear that you have come to the end of so long a journey without mishap, and that you have scorned the lure of Paris and made such haste to reach a place in which you can enjoy cultured leisure and the company of learned men. It is much to your credit that you have done so. As long as you remain there you will be in safe harbour; elsewhere you will find yourself endangered by the Syrtes, the Rocks, and the Sirens' voices. At the same time I would not have you drink too deep of the wine of Saumur, which you hope to enjoy, unless you are careful to dilute the vintage of Liber with a more liberal measure of water from the Muses' spring, in the proportion of more than five parts to one. But you have the best of advisers on this subject, and do not need a word from me. You will find it to your own best interest to obey him, and will at the same time give the greatest satisfaction to your excellent mother and earn a constant increase of her affection for you. That you may be enabled to do this should be your daily prayer to Almighty God.

Farewell, and see that you return to us with as great an increase of virtue and of culture as possible; that will give the greatest possible satisfaction to me in particular.

Westminster, August 1st, 1657

26 *To* the most distinguished MR HENRY DE BRASS

I AM later than I intended in writing to you, because various engagements have stood in my way during the last few days. I was the more anxious to reply promptly, because your letter, so full of learning, gave me an obvious opportunity of offering you not so much advice (which I think you ask out of compliment to me rather than for any real use it may be to yourself), as congratulation. And above all I congratulate myself on my good fortune in having, as it seems, explained the meaning of Sallust to such good purpose, and you on having read so carefully and with so much profit the works of that judicious author. Of him I would say to you, as Quintilian said of Cicero, that he who appreciates Sallust may be sure of having made considerable progress in history.

As regards that precept of Aristotle in the third book of the *Rhetoric*, of which you ask for an explanation, "Use should be made of maxims in the narrative and in the pleading, for this has an ethical effect", it appears to me to need little comment, except that "narrative" and "pleading" (for which the term "proof" is also used) must here be understood as applying to rhetorical, and not to historical, composition. For the functions of an orator and of an historian are different, whether in the narrative or in the proof, just as the art of Rhetoric is different from that of History. The methods proper to an historian can be learned better from ancient authors such as Polybius, Dionysius of Halicarnassus, Diodorus, Cicero, Lucian, and many others like them, in whose works we may find here and there a few precepts on this subject.

I wish you all good fortune and safety in your studies and your travels, and a success so well deserved by the spirit and diligence which, as I see, you show in all honourable pursuits. Farewell.

Westminster, December 16*th,* 1657

27 *To* the accomplished PETER HEIMBACH

I HAVE received your letter dated the Hague, December 18th. As I see your interests demand it, I hasten to reply on the very day on which I received it. In it you first thank me for some kindness or other, which I only wish were of real value, as I take the deepest interest in your affairs; you then ask me to give you an introduction to our Minister appointed to Holland, through Lord Lawrence. I much regret that this is not in my power. I have small acquaintance with men of influence, since I am much confined to my house, as indeed I prefer to be. Besides, I understand that he has already embarked and is nearly at his destination, and moreover has with him the man he intends to appoint as his secretary, the very post you wish to obtain.

But the post is this instant leaving. Farewell.

Westminster, December 18*th,* 1657

28 *To* JEAN LABADIE, Minister of the Church of Orange

IN being so late in replying to you, most excellent and reverend Sir, I feel sure that our friend Durie will not refuse to take the blame for my delay upon himself. For as soon as he had communicated to me that paper, which you wished to have read to me, giving an account of your doings and sufferings on behalf of the Gospel, I lost no time in preparing this letter to you. I particularly wished to give it to the first messenger to leave, since I was anxious as to the construction you would put upon my long silence.

Meanwhile I am most grateful to your friend Du Moulin of Nîmes, who has procured me the goodwill of many good men in those parts by his kind words and friendly commendation of me. I am indeed fully aware that I have obtained a considerable reputation far and wide, either because I did not shrink, when publicly commissioned, from the contest with an adversary of such repute, or because of the general interest in the subject, or lastly on account of the style of the composition. Yet it is my conviction that the only real fame I can claim is the good opinion held of me by good men. You have made it perfectly clear that you share this view, for your zeal and devotion to Christian truth have inspired you to endure many labours and sustain the assaults of many adversaries; moreover you show the utmost courage in your daily conduct, by which, far from courting the applause of the unregenerate, you dare to incur their inevitable dislike and ill-will. Happy that you are, in being singled out by God from so many thousands of men, wise and learned men too, to be snatched from the very gates and jaws of Hell and called to such noble and courageous testimony to the Gospel!

I have just found reason to think that it was by the special interposition of Providence that I did not reply to you earlier. I understood from your letter that you were assailed and beset on every hand by bitter foes, and were seeking, as well you might, some refuge to which you might retire in the last resort, if that should prove necessary, and that your choice had fallen upon England. I rejoiced for more reasons than one that you had come to this decision; one reason being the hope of having you here, and another my happiness that you should hold so high an opinion of my country. At the same time I was distressed at not being able, at that time, to see how fitting provision could be made for you here, especially as you do not know English. But now most fortunately it happens that a certain French minister of great age passed away a few days ago. The most influential men in that congregation, knowing that you are far from safe where you are, are most anxious to have you chosen to succeed him, and do indeed extend that invitation to you. (This I tell you not on mere hearsay, but on the information of the persons concerned.) They have decided to defray the expenses of your journey, and to provide you with a living as good as that of any French minister in England. They also assure you that you shall want for nothing which could contribute to the pleasant discharge of your pastoral duties among them. Therefore take my advice, reverend Sir, and hasten at once to those who desire your presence so much, and to a place in which you will reap a harvest, not perhaps over-rich in this world's goods, but, I hope, rich in the number of souls you may save, which is what such men as you desire above all. Rest assured that you will be most warmly welcomed by all good men; and the sooner you come the happier they will be. Farewell.

Westminster, April 21st, 1659

29 *To* HENRY OLDENBURG

THE pardon which you ask for your silence you must rather extend to mine, for it was, if I remember rightly, my turn to write. I have been prevented not by any diminution of my regard for you (of this I beg you to be assured), but by other occupations or domestic cares; or possibly my own lack of energy for writing has laid me open to the charge of neglecting my duty.

In reply to your enquiries, I am, thank God, as well as usual. I have no intention of composing a history of our troubles, as you appear to urge me to do, for it is better to pass them over in silence than to proclaim them abroad; and we do not so much need someone to write a history of them as someone able successfully to settle these troubles themselves. Like you, I am afraid that this civil discord, or rather madness, will leave us too much at the mercy of the enemies of liberty and of religion, who have lately joined forces. Yet they can inflict no deeper wound upon religion than we have ourselves already inflicted by our wickedness.

But I hope that God will not permit the machinations and assaults of our enemies to succeed as they desire, on His own account and for His own glory, which is now at stake, whatever disorders kings and cardinals may plot and devise.

Meanwhile, I pray that the Protestant Synod of Loudun, which is, as you tell me, to meet shortly, may have what no other synod has yet had, a happy issue, not like that in which Nazianzen took part. The issue of this one will be happy enough if, even should it decree nothing else, it should decree the expulsion of Morus.

Be good enough to give me the earliest information of my posthumous adversary, as soon as he makes his appearance. Farewell. *Westminster, December 20th,* 1659

30 *To* the noble youth RICHARD JONES

YOU send me most modest apologies for the long break in your correspondence with me, though you might with more reason accuse me of the same fault. I hardly know whether I should prefer your not having committed the offence to your having made such an apology as this. On no account allow yourself to imagine that I measure your gratitude (if indeed you owe me any) by the regularity of your letters. You can best prove your gratitude to me by showing the results of those services of mine to you, of which you speak, not so much in the frequency of your letters as in your steady devotion to noble pursuits and in the merits of your conduct.

You have done well to set out on the road to virtue while studying at your present training-school abroad. But you must realise that so far the roads to vice and to virtue are one; you must now go on to the parting of the ways. And you must now make ready betimes to leave the pleasant and flowery road common to both, and to climb that steep and rugged ascent which leads to virtue alone, willingly and of your own choice, though beset by difficulty and danger.

You have great advantages over others in this task, believe me, in having the aid of so faithful and experienced a guide. Farewell.

Westminster, December 20th, 1659

31   *To* the accomplished PETER HEIMBACH, Councillor to the Elector of Brandenburg

So many of my countrymen have perished in this tragic year of plague that I am not at all surprised if, as you say, you believed a particular rumour that I too had been carried off. I cannot be altogether displeased that such a rumour was current among your fellow-countrymen, as it seems to have been, if it sprang from their interest in my welfare. But I am still alive and well, by the grace of God, Who had prepared a refuge for me in the country. And I pray that I may not yet be found altogether useless for any task which still remains for me to perform in this life.

I am delighted to find that you have remembered me after so long a time, although, to judge by your elaborate compliments, there seems some reason to suspect that you do not remember me very clearly, since you express your admiration for the union in my person of so many virtues which are incompatible. For my part, I should dread too large a family as the result of so many unions, if it were not common knowledge that virtues grow and flourish best in poverty and hardships. One of those virtues, however, has not requited me very handsomely for my hospitality. For the virtue you call statesmanship (but which I would rather have you call loyalty to my country), after captivating me with her fair-sounding name, has, so to speak, almost left me without a country. However, the chorus of the others makes a fine harmony. One's country is wherever it is well with one.

I will close by begging you to lay the blame for any faults in spelling or lack of punctuation you may notice upon the boy who writes this at my dictation, and who knows no Latin at all. I am obliged, much to my annoyance, to spell out the letters one by one as I dictate.

For the rest, I am very glad that the merits, the

promise of which I recognised in you as a young man, have raised you to so honourable a place in your Prince's favour; and I wish you all good fortune in all else and trust it will be yours. Farewell.

London, August 15*th,* 1666

SOME OF THE AUTHOR'S PRELIMINARY ACADEMIC EXERCISES

1 Delivered in College

Whether Day or Night is the more excellent

IT is a frequent maxim of the most eminent masters of rhetoric, as you know well, Members of the University, that in every style of oration, whether demonstrative, deliberative, or judicial, the speaker must begin by winning the good-will of his audience; without it he cannot make any impression upon them, nor succeed as he would wish in his cause. If this be so (and, to tell the truth, I know that the learned are all agreed in regarding it as an established axiom), how unfortunate I am and to what a pass am I brought this day! At the very outset of my oration I fear I shall have to say something contrary to all the rules of oratory, and be forced to depart from the first and chief duty of an orator. For how can I hope for your good-will, when in all this great assembly I encounter none but hostile glances, so that my task seems to be to placate the implacable? So provocative of animosity, even in the home of learning, is the rivalry of those who pursue different studies or whose opinions differ concerning the studies they pursue in common. However, I care not if "Polydamas and the women of Troy prefer Labeo to me;—a trifle this".

Yet to prevent complete despair, I see here and there, if I do not mistake, some who without a word show clearly by their looks how well they wish me. The approval of these, few though they be, is more precious to me than that of the countless hosts of the ignorant, who lack all intelligence, reasoning power, and sound judgment, and who pride themselves on the ridiculous effervescing froth of their verbiage. Stripped of their covering of patches borrowed from new-fangled authors, they will prove to have no more in them than a serpent's slough, and once they have come to the end of their stock of phrases you will find them unable to utter so much as a syllable, for all the world like dumb men or the frogs of Seriphus. How difficult Heraclitus would find it, were he still alive, to keep a straight face at the sight of these speechifiers (if I may call them so without offence), first grandly spouting their lines in the tragic part of Euripides' Orestes, or as the mad Hercules in his dying agony, and then, their slender stock of phrases exhausted and their glory all gone, drawing in their horns and crawling off like snails.

But to return to the point, from which I have wandered a little. If there is anyone who has refused peace on any terms and declared war *à mort* against me, I will for once stoop to beg and entreat him to lay aside his animosity for a moment and show himself an unbiassed judge in this debate, and not to allow the speaker's fault (if such there be) to prejudice the best and most deserving of causes. If you consider that I have spoken with too much sharpness and bitterness, I confess that I have done so intentionally, for I wish the beginning of my speech to resemble the first gleam of dawn, which presages the fairest day when overcast.

The question whether Day or Night is preferable is no common theme of discussion, and it is now my duty, the task meted out to me this morning, to probe the subject thoroughly and radically, though it might seem better suited to a poetical exercise than to a contest of rhetoric.

Did I say that Night had declared war on Day? What should this portend? What means this daring enterprise? Are the Titans waging anew their ancient war, and renewing the battle of Phlegra's plain? Has Earth

54

brought forth new offspring of portentous stature to flout the gods of heaven? Or has Typhoeus forced his way from beneath the bulk of Etna piled upon him? Or last, has Briareus eluded Cerberus and escaped from his fetters of adamant? What can it possibly be that has now thrice roused the hopes of the gods of hell to rule the empire of the heavens? Does Night so scorn the thunderbolt of Jove? Cares she nothing for the matchless might of Pallas, which wrought such havoc in days of old among the earth-born brothers? Has she forgotten Bacchus' triumph over the shattered band of Giants, renowned through all the space of heaven? No, none of these. Full well she remembers, to her grief, how of those brothers most were slain by Jove, and the survivors driven in headlong flight even to the furthest corners of the underworld. Not for war, but for something far other, does she now anxiously prepare. Her thoughts now turn to complaints and accusations, and, womanlike, after a brave fight with tooth and nail, she proceeds to argument or rather abuse, to try, I suppose, whether her hands or her tongue are the better weapon. But I will soon show how baseless, how arrogant, and how ill-founded is her claim to supremacy, compared with Day's. And indeed I see Day herself, awakened by the crowing of the cock, hastening hither more swiftly than is her wont, to hear her own praise.

Now since it is generally agreed that to be of noble lineage and to trace one's descent back to kings or gods of old is an essential qualification for honours and dignity, it behoves us to enquire, first, which of the two is of nobler birth, secondly, which can trace back her descent the furthest, and thirdly, which is of the greater service to mankind?

I find it stated by the most ancient authorities on mythology that Demogorgon, the ancestor of all the gods (whom I suppose to be identical with the Chaos of the ancients), was the father of Earth, among his many children. Night was the child of Earth, by an unknown father, (though Hesiod gives a slightly different pedigree and calls Night the child of Chaos, in the line "From Chaos sprang Erebus and black Night"). Whatever her parentage, when she had reached marriageable age, the shepherd Phanes asked her to wife. Her mother consented, but she herself opposed the match, refusing to contract an alliance with a man she did not know and had never seen, and one moreover whose style of life was so different from her own. Annoyed at the rebuff, and with his love turned to hatred, Phanes in his indignation pursued this dusky daughter of Earth through all the length and breadth of the world to slay her. She now feared his enmity as much as she had previously scorned his love. Therefore she did not feel secure enough even among the most distant peoples or in the most remote places, nor even in the very bosom of her mother, but fled for refuge, secretly and by stealth, to the incestuous embrace of her brother Erebus. Thus she found at once a release from her pressing fears and a husband who was certainly very like herself. From this pretty pair Aether and Day are said to have sprung, according to Hesiod, whom I have already quoted:

> From Night again sprang Aether and the Day
> Whom she conceived and bore by Erebus' embrace.

But the more cultured Muses and Philosophy herself, the neighbour of the gods, forbid us to place entire confidence in the poets who have given the gods their forms, especially the Greek poets; and no one should regard it as a reproach to them that in a question of such importance they hardly seem sufficiently reliable authorities. For if any of them has departed from the truth to some slight extent, the blame should not be laid upon their genius, which is most divine, but upon the perverse and blind ignorance of the age, which at that time was all-pervading. They have attained an ample meed of honour and of glory by gathering together in one place and forming into organised communities men who previously roamed like beasts at random through the forests and mountains, and by being the first to teach, by their divine inspiration, all the sciences which are known to-day, arraying them in the charming cloak of fable; and their best title to everlasting fame (and that no mean one) is that they have left to their successors the full development of that knowledge of the Arts which they so happily began.

Do not then, whoever you are, hastily accuse me of disregarding and altering the statements of all the ancient poets, without any authority to support me. For I am not taking upon myself to do that, but am only attempting to bring them to the test of reason, and thereby to examine whether they can bear the scrutiny of strict truth.

First, then, the story that makes Night the child of Earth is a learned and elegant allegory of antiquity; for what is it that makes night envelop the world but the dense and solid earth, coming between the sun's light and our horizon?

Then, as to the statements of the mythologists, calling Night sometimes fatherless, sometimes motherless, these too are pleasing fictions, if we understand them to signify that she was a bastard or a changeling, or else that her parents refused for very shame to acknowledge so infamous and ignoble a child. But why they should believe that Phanes, endowed as he was with a wondrous and superhuman beauty, was so much in love with Night, a mere mulatto or silhouette, as even to wish to marry her, seems a problem hopelessly difficult to solve, unless the phenomenal scarcity of females at that time left him no choice.

But now let us come to close quarters with our subject. The ancients interpret Phanes as the sun or the day, and in relating that he at first sought Night in marriage and then pursued her to avenge his rejection, they mean only to signify the alternation of day and night. But why should they have thought it necessary, in order to show this, to represent Phanes as a suitor for the hand of Night, when their perpetual alternation and mutual repulsion, as it were, could be indicated far better by the figure of an innate and unremitting hatred? for it is well known that light and darkness have been divided from one another by an implacable hatred from the very beginning of time. It is in fact my opinion that Night got her Greek name of εὐφρόνη for the very reason that she showed caution and good sense in refusing to bind herself in wedlock to Phanes; for if she had once submitted to his embrace she would doubtless have been destroyed by his beams and by his unendurable radiance, and either annihilated altogether or utterly consumed by fire; like Semele, who, legend says, perished by fire, against the will of her lover Jove. For this reason, with a proper regard for her security, she preferred Erebus to Phanes. With reference to this, Martial aptly and wittily says, "Worst of husbands, worst of wives, I wonder not that you agree so well".

It is, I think, proper to mention with what a handsome family, how like their mother, she presented her husband—namely Misery, Envy, Fear, Deceit, Fraud, Obstinacy, Poverty, Want, Hunger, Fretfulness, Sickness, Old Age, Pallor, Darkness, Sleep, Death, and Charon, her last child; so that the proverb *tel arbre, tel fruit* is exactly applicable to this case.

There are, however, some who maintain that Night also bore Aether and Day to her husband Erebus. But who in his senses would not howl down and turn out the advocate of such a theory, as he would anyone who seriously propounded Democritus' notions or the fairy-tales of childhood? Is it indeed probable on the face of it that black and gloomy Night should be the mother of a child so comely, so sweet, so universally beloved and desired? Such a child, as soon as conceived, would have caused her mother's death by her birth before due time, would have driven her father Erebus into headlong flight, and forced old Charon to hide his dazzled eyes beneath the waters of the Styx and flee to seek what refuge he might in the realms below, as fast as his oars and sails could carry him. No, so far from being born in Hades, Day has never even shown her face there, nor can she find entrance even through a chink or cranny, except in defiance of Fate's decree. Nay, I dare rather declare that Day is older than Night, and that when the world had but newly emerged from Chaos, Day shed her wide-spreading rays over it, before ever the turn of Night had come—unless indeed we are so perverse as to call by the name of Night that foul and murky darkness, or regard it as identical with Demogorgon.

Therefore I hold that Day is the eldest daughter of Heaven, or rather of his son, begotten by him, it is said, to be the comfort of the race of men and the terror of the infernal gods, for fear lest Night should rule unopposed, lest Ghosts and Furies and all that loathsome brood of monsters, unchecked by any barrier between Earth and Hades, should leave the pit of Hell and make their way even to the upper world, and lest wretched Man, enveloped and surrounded by murky darkness, should suffer even in this life the tortures of the damned.

So far, Members of the University, I have endeavoured to drag from their deep and dark hiding-places the obscure children of Night; you will immediately perceive how worthy they are of their parentage—especially if I should first devote the best of my small powers to the praise of Day—though Day herself must far transcend the eloquence of all who sing her praise.

In the first place, there is assuredly no need to describe to you how welcome and how desirable Day is to every living thing. Even the birds cannot hide their delight, but leave their nests at peep of dawn and noise it abroad from the tree-tops in sweetest song, or darting upwards as near as they may to the sun, take their flight to welcome the returning day. First of all these the wakeful cock acclaims the sun's coming, and like a herald bids mankind shake off the bonds of sleep, and rise and run with joy to greet the new-born day. The kids skip in the meadows, and beasts of every kind leap and gambol in delight. The sad heliotrope, who all night long has gazed toward the east, awaiting her beloved Sun, now smiles and beams at her lover's approach. The marigold too and rose, to add their share to the joy of all, open their petals and shed abroad their perfume, which they have kept for the Sun alone, and would not give to Night, shutting themselves up within their little leaves at fall of evening. And all the other flowers raise their heads, drooping and weighed down with dew, and offer themselves to the Sun, mutely begging him to kiss away the tear-drops which his absence brought. The Earth too decks herself in lovelier robes to honour the Sun's coming, and the clouds, arrayed in garb of every hue, attend the rising god in festive train and long procession. And last, that nothing may be lacking to proclaim his praise, the Persians and the Libyans give him divine honours; the Rhodians too have dedicated to his glory that far-famed Colossus of astounding size, created by the miraculous art of Chares of Lindus; to the Sun too, we are told, the Indians even to this day make sacrifice with incense and with every kind of pomp. You yourselves, Members of the University, must bear witness how delightful, how welcome, how long-awaited is the light of morning, since it recalls you to the cultured Muses from whom cruel Night parted you still unsatisfied and athirst. Saturn, hurled down to Hades from highest heaven, bears witness how gladly he would return to the light of day from that dread gloom, would Jove but grant the boon. Lastly, it is manifest that Pluto himself far preferred light to his own kingdom of darkness, since he so often strove to gain the realm of heaven. Thus Orpheus says with truth and with poetic skill in his hymn to Dawn—"Then of a truth do mortal men rejoice, nor is there one who flees thy face which shines above, when thou dost shake sweet sleep from their eyes. Every man is glad, and every creeping thing, all the tribes of beast and bird, and all the many creatures of the deep".

Nor is this to be wondered at, when we reflect that Day serves for use as well as pleasure, and is alone fitted to further the business of life; for who would have the hardihood to sail the wide and boundless seas, without a hope that Day would dawn? He would cross the ocean even as the ghosts cross Lethe and Acheron, beset on every hand by the fearsome darkness. Every man would then pass his life in his own mean hovel, hardly daring even to creep outside, so that the dissolution of human society must needs follow. To no purpose would Apelles have pictured Venus rising from the waves, in vain would Zeuxis have painted Helen, if dark, dense night hid from our eyes these wondrous sights. In vain too would the earth bring forth in abundance vines twining in many a winding trail, in vain nobly towering trees; in vain would she deck herself anew with buds and blossoms, as with stars, striving to imitate the heaven above. Then indeed that noblest of the senses, sight, would lose its use to every creature; yes, and the light of the world's eye being quenched, all things would fade and perish utterly; nor would the men who dwelt upon the darkened earth long survive this tragedy, since nothing would be left to support their life, nor any means of staying the lapse of all things into the primeval Chaos.

One might continue in this strain with unabating flow, but Day herself in modesty would not permit the full recital, but would hasten her downward course toward the sunset to check her advocate's extravagances. My day is now indeed already drawing to its close, and will soon give place to night, to prevent your saying in jest that this is the longest day though the season is midwinter. This alone I ask, that by your leave I may add a few words which I cannot well omit.

With good reason, then, have the poets declared that

Night springs from Hell, since by no means whatever could so many grievous ills descend upon mankind from any other quarter. For when night falls all things grow foul and vile, no difference can then be seen between a Helen and Canidia, a precious jewel and a common stone (but that some gems have power to outlive the darkness). Then too the loveliest spots strike horror to the heart, a horror gathering force from a silence deep and sad. All creatures lingering in the fields, be they man or beast, hasten to house or lair for refuge; then, hiding their heads beneath their coverings, they shut their eyes against the dread aspect of Night. None may be seen abroad save thieves and rogues who fear the light, who, breathing murder and rapine, lie in wait to rob honest folk of their goods, and wander forth by night alone, lest day betray them. For Day lays bare all crimes, nor ever suffers wrongdoing to pollute her light. None will you meet save ghosts and spectres, and fearsome goblins who follow in Night's train from the realms below; it is their boast that all night long they rule the earth and share it with mankind. To this end, I think, night sharpens our hearing, that our ears may catch the sooner and our hearts perceive with greater dread the groans of spectres, the screeching of owls and night-birds, and the roaring of lions that prowl in search of prey. Hence clearly is revealed that man's deceit who says that night brings respite from their fears to men and lulls every care to rest. How false and vain is this opinion they know well from their own bitter experience who have ever felt the pangs of guilty consciences; they are beset by Sphinxes and Harpies, Gorgons and Chimaeras, who hunt their victims down with flaming torches in their hands.

Those poor wretches too know it full well who have no friend to help or succour them, none to assuage their grief with words of comfort, but must pour out their useless plaints to senseless stones, longing and praying for the dawn of day. For this reason did that choicest poet Ovid call Night the mighty foster-mother of cares.

Some indeed say that it is above all by night that our bodies, broken and worn out by the labours of the day, are revived and restored. But this is the merciful ordinance of God, for which we owe no gratitude to Night. But even were it so, sleep is not a thing so precious that Night deserves honour for the bestowal of it. For when we betake ourselves to sleep, we do in truth but confess ourselves poor and feeble creatures, whose puny frames cannot endure even a little while without repose. And, to be sure, what is sleep but the image and semblance of death? Hence in Homer Sleep and Death are twins, conceived together and born at a single birth.

Lastly, it is thanks to the sun that the moon and the other stars display their fires by night, for they have no light to radiate but such as they borrow from the sun.

Who then but a son of darkness, a robber, a gamester, or one whose wont it is to spend his nights in the company of harlots and snore away his days—who, I ask, but such a fellow would have undertaken to defend a cause so odious and discreditable? I wonder that he dare so much as look upon this sun, or share with other men, without a qualm, that light which he is slandering so ungratefully. He deserves to share the fate of Python, slain by the stroke of the sun's hostile rays. He deserves to pass a long and loathsome life imprisoned in Cimmerian darkness. He deserves, above all, to see sleep overcoming his hearers even as he speaks, so that his best eloquence affects them no more than an idle dream, till, drowsy himself, he is cheated into taking his hearers' nods and snores for nods of approval and murmurs of praise as he ends his speech.

But I see the black brows of Night, and note the advance of darkness; I must withdraw, lest Night overtake me unawares.

I beg you then, my hearers, since Night is but the passing and the death of Day, not to give Death the preference over Life, but graciously to honour my cause with your votes; so may the Muses prosper your studies, and Dawn, the friend of the Muses, hear your prayers; and may the Sun, who sees and hears all things, hearken to all in this assembly who honour and support his cause. I have done.

2   Delivered in the Public Schools

On the Harmony of the Spheres

IF there is any room for an insignificant person like myself, Members of the University, after you have heard so many eminent speakers, I too will attempt, to the best of my small powers, to show my appreciation of this day's solemn celebrations, and to follow, though at a distance, the festal train of eloquence to-day. And so, though I should in any case shun and avoid the usual trite and hackneyed topics, I am fired and aroused to do my utmost to find some novel theme by the thought of this day's importance and of our speakers who, as was to be expected, have already paid such worthy tribute to it. These two considerations might well suffice to stimulate and spur on even a dull and sluggish brain. So I conceived the idea of making a few preliminary remarks with open hand, as we say, and rhetorical exuberance, on the subject of that heavenly harmony which is presently to be discussed as it were with closed fist—but this with an eye to the time at my disposal, which is now strictly limited.

Now I beg you, my hearers, not to take this theory as seriously intended. For who in his senses would suppose that Pythagoras, a very god among philosophers, whose name all men of that time hailed with the most profound reverence—who, I ask, would suppose that he had ever put forward a theory based on such very poor foundations? Surely, if he held any doctrine of the harmony of the spheres, or taught that the heavens revolve in unison with some sweet melody, it was only as a means of suggesting allegorically the close interrelation of the orbs and their uniform revolution in accordance with the laws of destiny for ever. In this he followed the example of the poets, or (what is almost the same thing) of the divine oracles, who never display before the eyes of the vulgar any holy or secret mystery unless it be in some way cloaked or veiled.

Pythagoras was followed by Plato, that best interpreter of Mother Nature; he tells us that upon each one of the celestial orbs is seated a being called a Siren, at whose mellifluous song both gods and men are rapt in wonder.

Homer moreover used the remarkable and apt metaphor of the golden chain suspended by Jove from heaven to represent this universal concord and sweet union of all things which Pythagoras poetically figures as harmony.

Then Aristotle, the rival and constant detractor of Pythagoras and Plato, wishing to construct a road to fame on the ruins of these great masters' theories, foisted on Pythagoras the literal doctrine of the unheard symphony of heaven and of the melody of the spheres. But if only fate or chance had allowed your soul, O Father Pythagoras, to transmigrate into my body, you would not have lacked a champion to deliver you without difficulty, under however heavy a burden of obloquy you might be labouring!

After all, we may well ask, why should not the heavenly bodies give forth musical tones in their annual revolutions? Does it not seem reasonable to you, Aristotle? Why, I can hardly believe that those Intelligences of yours could have endured through so many centuries the sedentary toil of making the heavens rotate, if the ineffable music of the stars had not prevented them from leaving their posts, and the melody, by its enchantment, persuaded them to stay. If you rob the heavens of this music, you devote those wonderful minds and subordinate gods of yours to a life of drudgery, and condemn them to the treadmill. And even Atlas himself would long since have cast down the burden of the skies from his shoulders to its ruin, had not that sweet harmony soothed him with an ecstasy of delight as he panted and sweated beneath his heavy load. And we may well believe that it is in order to tune their own notes in accord with that harmony of heaven to which they listen so intently, that the lark takes her flight up into the clouds at daybreak and the nightingale passes the lonely hours of night in song.

Hence arose the story, which has prevailed since the earliest times, of how the Muses dance before Jove's altar day and night; hence too the attribution to Phoebus, in the remote past, of musical skill. Hence the belief held by revered antiquity that Harmonia was the daughter of Jove and Electra, and that at her marriage to Cadmus all the choirs of heaven sang in concert.

What if no one on earth has ever heard this symphony of the stars? It does not therefore follow that everything beyond the sphere of the moon is mute and utterly benumbed in silence. The fault is in our own deaf ears, which are either unable or unworthy to hear these sweet strains.

But this melody is not all unheard. For who, O Aristotle, could believe that those goats you tell of keep skipping in the midmost tracts of air for any other reason than that when they plainly hear the orchestra of heaven, being so near at hand, they cannot choose but dance?

Again, Pythagoras alone among men is said to have heard this music—if indeed he was not rather some good spirit and denizen of heaven, sent down perchance by the gods' behest to instruct mankind in holiness and lead them back to righteousness; at the least, he was assuredly a man endowed with a full meed of virtue, worthy to hold converse with the gods themselves,

66

whose like he was, and to partake of the fellowship of heaven. Therefore I wonder not if the gods, who loved him well, permitted him to share the most secret mysteries of nature.

The fact that we are unable to hear this harmony seems certainly to be due to the presumption of that thief Prometheus, which brought so many evils upon men, and robbed us of that happiness which we may never again enjoy so long as we remain buried in sin and degraded by brutish desires; for how can we become sensitive to this heavenly sound while our souls are, as Persius says, bowed to the ground and lacking in every heavenly element? But if our souls were pure, chaste, and white as snow, as was Pythagoras' of old, then indeed our ears would ring and be filled with that exquisite music of the stars in their orbits; then would all things turn back to the Age of Gold, and we ourselves, free from every grief, would pass our lives in a blessed peace which even the gods might envy.

At this point time cuts me short in mid career, and luckily too, for I am afraid that by my confused and unmelodious style I have been all this while offending against that very harmony of which I speak, and have myself been an obstacle to your hearing it. And so I have done.

3   Delivered in the Public Schools

An Attack on the Scholastic Philosophy

I HAVE been deeply occupied of late, gentlemen, in seeking, and indeed one of my chief anxieties has been to find, what device of rhetoric would best enable me to engage my hearers' attention: when of a sudden there came into my mind the precept often inculcated in his writings by Cicero (with whose name my speech auspiciously begins)—namely that the fundamental duties of an orator are first to instruct, secondly to delight, and thirdly to persuade.

Now for instruction, it ill befits me to take upon myself to give it to men so erudite in every branch of learning as yourselves, or you to receive it; still, it may be permissible for me to take the nearest course and bring to your notice a matter which may prove to be not altogether without interest. Secondly for delight, though I greatly fear it is beyond my poor abilities, yet it shall be my chief wish to afford this also: but even if I attain this, it will not be enough unless I succeed also in persuading you. Thirdly for persuasion, I shall attain the height of my ambition for the present if I can induce you who hear me to turn less assiduously the pages of those vast and ponderous tomes of our professors of so-called exactitude, and to be less zealous in your study of the crabbed arguments of wiseacres.

Now to make it plain to all how proper and reasonable is my theme, I will show briefly, in the short half hour at my disposal, that these studies promote neither delight nor instruction, nor indeed do they serve any useful purpose whatsoever.

First I will issue a challenge, gentlemen. If I can at all judge your feelings by my own, what pleasure can there possibly be in these petty disputations of sour old men, which reek, if not of the cave of Trophonius, at any rate of the monkish cells in which they were written, exude the gloomy severity of their writers, bear the traces of their authors' wrinkles, and in spite of their condensed style produce by their excessive tediousness only boredom and distaste; and if ever they are read at length, provoke an altogether natural aversion and an utter disgust in their readers. Many a time, when the duty of tracing out these petty subtleties for a while has been laid upon me, when my mind has been dulled and my sight blurred by continued reading—many a time, I say, I have paused to take breath, and have sought some slight relief from my boredom in looking to see how much yet remained of my task. When, as always happened, I found that more remained to be done than I had as yet got through, how often have I wished that instead of having these fooleries forced upon me I had been set to clean out the stable of Augeas again, and I have envied Hercules his luck in having been spared such labours as these by a kindly Juno.

And then this dull and feeble subject-matter, which as it were crawls along the ground, is never raised or elevated by the ornaments of style, but the style itself is dry and lifeless, so exactly suited to the barrenness of the subject that it might well have been composed in the reign of the gloomy king Saturn, but that the innocent simplicity of those days would have known nothing of the delusions and digressions with which these books abound in every part. Believe me, my learned friends, when I go through these empty quibbles as I often must, against my will, it seems to me as if I were forcing my way through rough and rocky wastes, desolate wildernesses, and precipitous mountain gorges. And so it is not likely that the dainty and elegant Muses preside over these ragged and tattered studies, or consent to be the patrons of their maudlin partisans; and I cannot believe that there was ever a place for them on Parnassus unless it were some waste corner at the very foot of the mountain, some spot with naught to commend it, tangled and matted with thorns and brambles, overgrown with thistles and nettles, remote from the dances and company of the goddesses, where no laurels grow nor flowers bloom, and to which the sound of Apollo's lyre can never penetrate.

Now surely divine poetry, by that power with which it is by heavenly grace indued, raises aloft the soul smothered by the dust of earth and sets it among the mansions of heaven, and breathing over it the scent of nectar and bedewing it with ambrosia instils into it heavenly felicity and whispers to it everlasting joy. Rhetoric, again, so captivates the minds of men and draws them after it so gently enchained that it has the power now of moving them to pity, now of inciting them to hatred, now of arousing them to warlike valour, now of inspiring them beyond the fear of death. History, skilfully narrated, now calms and soothes the restless and troubled mind, now fills it with delight, and now brings tears to the eyes; soft and gentle tears, tears which bring with them a kind of mournful joy. But these barren and useless controversies and bickerings lack all power to affect the emotions in any way whatever; they merely dull and stupefy the intellect. Further, they bring delight to none but those of a rude and boorish disposition, inclined by some innate tendency to quarrels and dissension, prating fellows moreover, and such as detest and ever turn away from sound and wholesome wisdom. Let us then banish such an one with all his quibbles to the Caucasus or wheresoever blind Barbarity holds sway; there let him set up his workshop of tricks and fallacies, and vex and torment himself to his heart's content about questions of no importance, until excessive fretting, like Prometheus' eagle, eats out his heart and consumes him altogether.

These studies are as fruitless as they are joyless, and can add nothing whatever to true knowledge. If we set before our eyes those hordes of old men in monkish garb, the chief authors of these quibbles, how many among them have ever contributed anything to the enrichment of literature? Beyond a doubt, by their harsh and uncouth treatment they have nearly rendered hideous that philosophy which was once cultured and well-ordered and urbane, and like evil genii they have implanted thorns and briars in men's hearts and introduced discord into the schools, which has wondrously retarded the happy progress of our scholars. For these quick-change philosophasters of ours argue back and forth, one bolstering up his thesis on every side, another labouring hard to cause its downfall, while what one would think firmly established by irrefragable argu-

ments is forthwith shattered by an opponent with the
greatest ease. Between them all the student hesitates,
as at a cross-roads, in doubt whither to turn or what
direction to choose, and unable to make any decision,
while such a host of weapons is hurled against him from
every side that they hide the light and shed deep darkness over the whole question; so that in the end the
reader is reduced to imitating the toils of Ceres and
seeking for Truth through all the world by the light of
a torch without ever finding it: at last he reaches such
a pitch of madness as to believe himself utterly blind
when in fact there is nothing for him to see.

Besides all this, it not infrequently happens that
those who have entirely devoted and dedicated themselves to this blight of disputation lamentably betray
their ignorance and absurd childishness when faced with
a new situation outside their usual idiotic occupation.
Finally, the supreme result of all this earnest labour is to
make you a more finished fool and cleverer contriver of
conceits, and to endow you with a more expert ignorance: and no wonder, since all these problems at which
you have been working in such torment and anxiety
have no existence in reality at all, but like unreal ghosts
and phantoms without substance obsess minds already
disordered and empty of all true wisdom.

For the rest, even were I silent, it is amply clear to
you how little these trivialities contribute to morality
or purity of life, which is the most important consideration of all. From this obviously follows my final point,
namely that this unseemly battle of words tends neither
to the general good nor to the honour and profit of our
country, which is generally considered the supreme
purpose of all sciences.

Now there are, as I have remarked, two things which
most enrich and adorn our country: eloquent speech
and noble action. But this contentious duel of words
has no power either to teach eloquence or to inculcate
wisdom or to incite to noble acts. Then away with these

ingenious praters, with all their forms and phrases, who
ought to be condemned after death to twist the rope in
Hades in company with the Ocnus of legend.

But how much better were it, gentlemen, and how
much more consonant with your dignity, now to let
your eyes wander as it were over all the lands depicted
on the map, and to behold the places trodden by the
heroes of old, to range over the regions made famous
by wars, by triumphs, and even by the tales of poets of
renown, now to traverse the stormy Adriatic, now to
climb unharmed the slopes of fiery Etna, then to spy
out the customs of mankind and those states which are
well-ordered; next to seek out and explore the nature
of all living creatures, and after that to turn your attention to the secret virtues of stones and herbs. And do
not shrink from taking your flight into the skies and
gazing upon the manifold shapes of the clouds, the
mighty piles of snow, and the source of the dews of
morning; then inspect the coffers wherein the hail is
stored and examine the arsenals of the thunderbolts.
And do not let the intent of Jupiter or of Nature elude
you, when a huge and fearful comet threatens to set the
heavens aflame, nor let the smallest star escape you of
all the myriads which are scattered and strewn between
the poles: yes, even follow close upon the sun in all his
journeys, and ask account of time itself and demand
the reckoning of its eternal passage.

But let not your mind rest content to be bounded and
cabined by the limits which encompass the earth, but
let it wander beyond the confines of the world, and at
the last attain the summit of all human wisdom and
learn to know itself, and therewith those holy minds and
intelligences whose company it must hereafter join.

What need I say more? In all these studies take as
your instructor him who is already your delight—Aristotle, who has recorded all these things with learning
and diligence for our instruction. I see that the mention
of his name at once arouses you, Members of the Uni-

versity, and that you are gradually being won over to my side, and following apace, as it were, at his invitation. If this be so, it is to him that you must render praise and thanks for any profit my words have brought; so far as concerns myself, I shall be well satisfied if you of your goodness grant me pardon for the length of my address.

4 Delivered in College

A THESIS

In the Destruction of any Substance there can be no Resolution into First Matter

THIS is not the place in which to enquire too nicely whether Error escaped from Pandora's box, or from the depths of the Styx, or lastly whether he is to be accounted one of the sons of Earth who conspired against the gods. This much, however, is clear to the least observant, that by imperceptible degrees, like Typhon of old or Neptune's son Ephialtes, he has grown to such portentous size that I believe Truth itself to be menaced by him. For I see that he often fights on equal terms against the goddess Truth, I see that after sustaining losses he is richer, after being wounded he is sound and whole, after being vanquished he is triumphant over his vanquishers, like the Libyan Antaeus in the ancient tale. So far has this gone, that one might with good reason doubt the correctness of Ovid's well-known poem, and question whether Astraea was really the last of the immortals to quit the earth; for I fear that many centuries later Peace and Truth too came to loathe mankind and abandoned it. For assuredly no one could be persuaded into believing that if Truth were still a visitor to the earth, one-eyed and near-sighted Error could look upon her, the co-equal of the sun, without being altogether blinded and cast back once more into that lower world from which he originally came forth.

But there can in fact be no doubt that Truth has fled away to her home in heaven, never to return to hapless man; and now foul Error reigns supreme in all the schools, and has seized the power, as it were, with the help of a strong and active body of supporters. With this added strength, and swollen past endurance, he has assailed every particle and fragment of natural philosophy and outraged it with impious claws, even as, we are told, the Harpies defiled the table of Phineus, King of Arcady.

The thing has come to such a pass that the richest dainties of philosophy, sumptuous as the feasts which the gods enjoy, now only disgust those who partake of them. For it often happens that a student who turns the pages of the philosophers' books and is busied about them day and night departs more puzzled than he came. For whatever one writer has affirmed and believes that he has established by a sufficient argument, another confutes, or at least seems to confute, with the greatest ease, and both are able almost indefinitely the one to find objections, the other replies. The wretched reader meanwhile, continually rent and torn in pieces as if between two wild beasts, and half dead with boredom, is at last left as at a cross-roads, without any idea which way to turn. But, to be quite candid, it may not be worth while to spend the trouble which is demanded in finding out on which side the truth really lies; for in fact it is very often about questions of the most trifling importance that the most heated disputes of the forces of philosophy occur.

But I seem to catch a whisper of "What is he driving at now? He attacks Error, while he himself wanders erratically all over the world". I confess that I have indeed erred and strayed, which I should not have done had I not hoped much from your kindness.

Well, I must now gird myself up to the task before me; and may the goddess Lua (as Lipsius says) grant me a happy deliverance from all my difficulties.

The problem which is set us to enucleate to-day is whether in the destruction of any substance there can be a resolution into first matter. This is usually expressed in others words, "whether any accidents which were in the corrupted substance remain also in that generated from it"—that is to say, whether when the form perishes all accidents which had previously existed in the composite perish also.

There is a wide divergence of opinion about this on the part of philosophers of great repute. Some vehemently assert that such a resolution does take place, others fight tooth and nail against its possibility. I am inclined to agree with these last, and am led to differ fundamentally from the former first by reason, as I believe, and secondly by the authority of so many eminent men. It remains for me shortly to attempt to supply a proof. I shall do so as briefly as possible, and first of all as follows.

If there is resolution into first matter, it follows that we are wrong in asserting the essential proposition with regard to first matter, namely that it is never found pure. Our opponents will hasten to reply: This is said in respect of form. Well, let us grant these sciolists that substantial forms are never found apart from accidental ones.

But this is a minor point, and does not go to the root of the question; we must use stronger arguments.

First then let us see whether we have any of the ancient philosophers on our side. Even as we ask, here comes Aristotle of his own accord to meet us, and ranges himself on our side, together with a chosen band of his commentators. And pray note, my hearers, that it was at Aristotle's own instance and instigation that this battle was begun, and that, I hope, under good auspices. He does in fact himself seem to hint at exactly our view, in *Metaph.* 7, *Text* 8, where he says that quantity is first of all inherent in matter. If anyone refuses to accept this dictum, I shall not hesitate to indict him for heresy, in accordance with the law of all the sages. Moreover, he elsewhere plainly regards quantity as a property of first matter, which most of his followers also assert; but who would tolerate the forcible separation of a property from its subject, even on the pronouncement of a judge appointed by themselves?

But now, let us come to close grips with the question, and weigh carefully what reason suggests.

The assertion, then, is proved first by the argument that matter has an actual proper entity in consequence of its own proper existence, and therefore is capable of having quantity, at any rate the quantity called indeterminate. There is also the argument sometimes confidently put forward that form is only received into matter through the medium of quantity.

Secondly, if an accident is destroyed, it can only be destroyed in one of the following ways—either by the introduction of a contrary, or by cessation of its term, or by the absence of some other conserving cause, or, lastly, by the defect of the proper subject in which it inheres. Quantity cannot be destroyed in the first way, since it has no contrary; the second way does not apply, since it is proper to relatives; nor by the absence of a conserving cause, for that which my opponents assign is form. Now accidents are conceived to depend upon form in two ways—in the genus of formal cause, or in that of efficient cause; the first kind of dependence is not immediate, for substantial form does not inform accidents, nor is it conceivable that a cause can have any other function in regard to them in this genus. Therefore it is only mediate, that is to say in so far as matter is dependent upon form, and quantity in turn on matter. The second kind of dependence is in the genus of efficient cause; but whether accidents are dependent on form or not in this genus is doubtful. But even if we grant that it is so, it still does not follow that when the form perishes the accidents also perish with it, because when that cause fails another similar one succeeds it immediately, which is completely sufficient to maintain precisely the same effect, and that without interruption. Finally, that quantity and other similar accidents are not annihilated by the defect of the proper subject is proved thus—the subject of quantity is either a composite or form or matter; now it is clear that it is not a composite, because an accident which is in a composite attains by its union both matter and form by means of one thing; but quantity cannot by any means attain a rational soul, for this is spiritual and entirely incapable of the formal effect of quantity, that is to say, of quantitative extension. Further, it is sufficiently clear from what has been said that form is not the subject of quantity. It follows therefore that only matter can be the subject of quantity, and so all inference of destruction is excluded in regard to quantity.

As regards the example of a scar commonly adduced, I consider it to be a very cogent argument; for no one could so force my credulity as to make me believe that it is quite other in the corpse than what it was just before in the living body, since there is neither reason nor necessity to correct our sense, which is indeed rarely deluded concerning its proper object. I would far rather listen to marvellous stories of ghosts and hobgoblins than to the foolish and futile yappings of these crazy philosophasters about the re-creation *de novo* of these accidents of theirs. Now we know for certain that heat and those other qualities of an animal which are capable of increase and decrease are precisely the same at the moment of death, and also after death; why then should these be destroyed when others like them are to be produced? Besides, if they were to be produced afresh they would not last so short a time, for they would not reach their utmost intensity suddenly, but only gradually and little by little. Remember too that it is a very ancient axiom that quantity follows matter and quality form.

I might indeed I ought to have dwelt longer on this

question. I cannot tell whether I have bored you, but I have certainly bored myself to extinction. It remains for me to deal with my opponents' arguments. May the Muses grant that I may reduce them to first matter, if that be possible, or rather to nothing at all.

As to their first point, Aristotle's testimony in saying that no sensible subject remains in generation, we reply that this should be understood as applying to the complete and integral subject, that is to say, to the substantial composite, as the ancient and learned author Philoponus bears witness. Secondly, regarding Aristotle's statement that matter is neither what, nor how much, nor of what kind; by this it is not meant that matter has no quantity nor quality, but that it does not include either quantity or quality of itself or in its own essence. Thirdly, Aristotle says that when the first substances are destroyed all accidents are destroyed. We do not deny that this will happen, provided you grant that another may immediately succeed that which was destroyed.

Finally, he says that form is received into pure matter; that is, by the purity of the substantial form.

Now the fight grows fierce, and victory hangs in the balance, for they renew the battle and attack us as follows: Since matter is pure potentiality, it has no being except that which it gains through the form it has borrowed; hence it has no power of itself to support accidents, unless at the least it is conjoined by nature to form, to which it is indebted for its being. This error they usually amend thus—that first matter has its own proper being, which may indeed be incomplete in the genus of substance, but as compared with accident may not unreasonably be called simply being. They object moreover that matter has regard to substantial form as its first act, but to accidents as its second act. I reply that matter has regard to form, first in the order of intention, but not of generation or execution. Our argument now begins to bubble and boil, and our opponents press harder upon us, as in mortal combat, as thus: Every property flows actively from the essence of that of which it is a property; but quantity cannot do so, for this flow is a form of activity, but matter has in itself no activity, being merely passive; therefore, etc., etc. I reply, that the natural combination of matter with quantity can be understood in two ways, first by reason of the passive potentiality alone within its own nature, which demands such an affection: for there is no necessity that every innate property should be attributed to a subject by reason of its active principle; since sometimes the passive suffices, in the way in which many consider that motion is natural to the heavens. Secondly, it can also be understood as being due to its intrinsic active flowing forth, since it contains in itself true and actual being.

But my opponents have not even yet lost all hope of victory; for they are making a second attack, inferring from this that form is combined with matter through the medium of quantity, since it is inherent in first matter. We, on the other hand, absolutely refuse to accept this inference, and in order to maintain our position unimpaired in spite of it, we draw this distinction, that form is combined with matter through the medium of quantity as a disposition or necessary condition, but not at all as a potentiality immediately receptive of form.

Finally, they argue thus: if quantity is inherent in matter alone, it follows that it is ingenerable and incorruptible; which seems to be contradictory, since movement in itself is toward quantity. However, we grant the inference, since in fact quantity is incorruptible as regards its own entity, but as regards its various terms it can begin and cease to be, by the conjunction and division of quantity; nor is motion in itself toward the production of quantity, but toward its accretion; and it does not exist by virtue of a new quantity coming into existence in nature, but by virtue of one quantity being subjoined to another, and by the quantity which was alien becoming proper to itself.

I might bring forward other arguments on both sides, but will refrain, to spare you boredom. At this point, then, it is best for me to beat a retreat.

5   Delivered in the Public Schools

There are no partial Forms in an Animal in addition to the Whole

THE Romans, masters of the world in ancient times, attained the highest summit of power, which neither the vastness of Assyria nor the martial prowess of Macedon could reach, and to which the majesty of kings in time to come will never be able to exalt itself. This position they attained, either because Jupiter, feeling the burden of his age and finding it enough for himself to rule over the heavens alone, wished to retire into private life, and therefore entrusted the reins of government over mankind to the Roman people, as being in some sort gods on earth; or because, when he cast his father Saturn down into Italy, he granted him this favour to console him for the loss of heaven, namely that his descendants the Romans should have dominion over the whole extent of land and ocean.

However this may be, he certainly did not allow them to enjoy this privilege without earning it, but only granted it to them after constant wars and prolonged toil; his intention being, I suppose, to prove whether the Romans were the only nation worthy to be the vice-gerents of supreme Jove on earth. And so they were compelled to live a life of abstinence and hardship, and to find the new pleasures of peace always cut short by war's alarms and the clash of arms around them. In addition to this, they were under the necessity of providing garrisons, which they had frequently to renew, for the various cities and provinces they had conquered, and of sending nearly all their young men either to distant wars or to their colonies. Moreover the victories they gained were not always bloodless; on the contrary, they often suffered grievous disasters. So for example Brennus, the leader of the Gauls, almost succeeded in destroying the glory of Rome in its early bloom, and the noble city of Carthage came within a little of wresting from Rome the governance of the world with which she had been divinely entrusted. Lastly, the Goths and Vandals under their king Alaric, and the Huns and Pannonians under their leaders Attila and Bleda passed in a torrent over the whole of Italy, cruelly plundered the abounding riches of the empire, the accumulated spoils of so many wars, overwhelmed in shameful flight the Romans, who were but now the lords of mankind, and captured the city, captured Rome herself, by the mere terror of their name. No deed in fact or fable could be more remarkable than this. It is as if victory herself had either fallen in love with them or been panic-stricken by their prowess in arms, so as to be completely at their command.

You have been wondering long enough, my hearers, what can be my reason for enlarging on all this; I will tell you. Whenever I consider and reflect upon these events, I am reminded afresh of the mighty struggle which has been waged to save Truth, and of the universal eagerness and watchfulness with which men are striving to rescue Truth, already tottering and almost overthrown, from the outrages of her foes. Yet we are powerless to check the inroads which the vile horde of errors daily makes upon every branch of learning. Error has indeed, by fair means or foul, gained such ascendancy as to be able to impose its own likeness on the snow-white form of heavenly Truth, and by I know not what artifice to assume her similitude. By this device, it seems, it has often deceived even great philosophers, and has laid claim to the honours and reverence which are due to Truth alone. This you will have an opportunity of seeing in the question at issue to-day, in which we find champions of no mean ability engaged, men who might win fair fame, if they would but abandon their present allegiance and serve under the banner of Truth.

So it is now my task to lay Error bare and to strip it of its borrowed plumes, thus reducing it to its native hideousness. To accomplish this the more readily, I think it best to follow in the footsteps of the weightiest authorities; for it is not to be expected that I should add anything of my own—anything, that is, which has escaped the notice and attention of so many men eminent for their learning. Therefore I will set forth briefly so much as is needed to elucidate the subject, and will add one or two arguments to fortify my position like a rampart. Then if there is any opposition or objection to my opinion, I will resolve it as best I may; but I will deal with all this in few words and only touch it, so to speak, with the tips of my wings.

We read that various opinions have been advanced in opposition to the idea of the unicity of form which the more discerning philosophers have always held to exist in one and the same matter. For some hotly assert that in an animal there may be several total forms, and this they maintain each according to his capacity; others roundly declare that though only one total form can be readily received by one and the same matter, yet several partial forms may be. For the moment I will make a truce with the former party, according to the usage of war, while I concentrate the whole strength and force of my attack upon the latter.

In the forefront let me set Aristotle, who is entirely on our side, and who, towards the end of the first book of the *De Anima*, unequivocally lends his support to our assertion.

No long investigation is needed to find a few more

arguments to add to this authority. Chrysostom Javello is the first to come to my help; from the dung-heap of his rude and unpolished style we may dig out gold and pearls; if anyone is so refined as to despise these, Aesop's fable of the cock will fit him very neatly. His argument runs much as follows: The distinction and organisation of dissimilar parts must precede the introduction of the soul, since this is the act not of any body at random, but of a physically organic body; therefore these partial forms must be corrupted immediately before the production of the total form, unless we are to disregard entirely the universally accepted axiom that "the generation of one thing is the corruption of another". The production of these partial forms is not followed by the instantaneous production of others similar to them; for this would be purposeless and at variance with the wisdom of Mother Nature. Secondly, since every form, whether perfect or imperfect, contributes its specific being, it necessarily follows that, as long as that form remains, that object also remains the same, not varied according to its substance; therefore the total form will supervene like an accident, that is to say not by generation but by alteration. It follows moreover that the soul of the whole, whether divisible or indivisible, is not sufficient to inform every part of the living creature fully and perfectly; this no reason can persuade us to grant. It also follows that one substantial form is as it were a proximate and permanent disposition toward another, which is contrary to truth, since every form constitutes an essence complete in the genus of substance. Finally, if there is a plurality of partial forms in every part, of a man for example, from them there will certainly arise one complete form distinct from the rational soul; hence this form will be the form either of an inanimate thing or corporeity, or of a mixture (which in fact is most unlikely to exist in man in addition to the soul); or else it will be a sensitive or vegetative soul. This latter assertion would be absolutely rejected by the more learned among the philosophers. I will refrain from further proof of this, since it is generally admitted and moreover does not go to the root of the matter.

Again, our opponents bring forward the objection (and this is the crux of the discussion) that when a part of an animal has been cut off it remains in act after the separation, not through the form of the whole, since it is outside the whole, nor through the form recently acquired, since there is no agent, no perceptible action, and no previous alteration; therefore it exists in act through the proper form which it had before, while it still formed a part of the whole. By this argument they consider that they batter down and utterly demolish our position. The reply which is commonly made is perfectly valid, that a form generated *de novo*, since it is of small account, as pertaining to a corpse and being as it were a way to resolution, certainly requires neither a long time, nor many dispositions, nor ordered alteration to be so generated. Besides, what if some other universal cause were to combine with the previous mixture to induce some kind of form, that there may not be pure and unqualified matter? Moreover, the fact that we can perceive manifold operations in an animal is not due to distinct partial forms but to the preponderance of the total soul, which is of equal importance with the forms distinct in appearance.

I would prefer to pass over, by agreement, the other minor objections which are put forward, for they are not vital, and will be more easily countered and more satisfactorily disproved if they chance to be brought forward in the course of the disputation.

Whatever the outcome may be, even if I fail in my cause, the cause itself will never fail. For invincible Truth has within herself strength enough and to spare for her own defence, and has no need of any other help; and though she may seem to us at times to be hard pressed and beaten to the ground, yet she maintains herself ever inviolate and uninjured by the claws of Error, even as the sun, who often shows himself to human eyes obscured and darkened by clouds, but then drawing in his beams and gathering together all his splendour, shines forth again in blazing glory without spot or stain.

6 Delivered in the College Summer Vacation, but in the Presence of almost the whole Body of Students, as is customary

(i) THE ORATION

Sportive Exercises on occasion are not inconsistent with philosophical Studies

ON my return from that city which is the chief of all cities, Members of the University, filled (I had almost said "to repletion") with all the good things which are to be found there in such abundance, I looked forward once more to enjoying a spell of cultured leisure, a mode of life in which, it is my belief, even the souls of the blessed find delight. I fully intended at last to bury myself in learning and to devote myself day and night to the charms of philosophy; for the alternation of toil and pleasure usually has the effect of annihilating the boredom brought about by satiety and of making us the more eager to resume our interrupted tasks. Just as I was warming to my work there came a sudden summons and I was dragged away by the yearly celebration of our ancient custom, and commanded to transfer that zeal, which I had intended to devote to the acquisition of knowledge, to foolery and the invention of new jests—as if the world were not already full of fools, as if that famous Ship of Fools, renowned in song like the Argo herself, had been wrecked, or finally as if there were not matter enough already to make even Democritus laugh.

But I ask your pardon, my hearers; for though I have spoken somewhat too freely, the custom which we celebrate to-day is assuredly no foolish one, but on the contrary most commendable, as I intend to make plain forthwith. And if Junius Brutus, that second founder of Rome and great avenger of the lusts of kings, could bring himself to disguise his almost godlike mind and wonderful natural talents under the semblance of idiocy, there is assuredly no reason why I should be ashamed to play the wise fool for a while, especially at the bidding of him whose duty it is, like the aediles' at Rome, to organise these shows, which are almost a ceremonial custom. I was further strongly induced and persuaded to undertake this office by the new-found friendliness towards me of you who are fellow-students of my own college. For when, some months ago, I was to make an academic oration before you, I felt sure that any effort of mine would have but a cold reception from you, and would find in Aeacus or Minos a more lenient judge than in any one of you. But quite contrary to my expectation, contrary indeed to any spark of hope I may have entertained, I heard, or rather I myself felt, that my speech was received with quite unusual applause on every hand, even on the part of those who had previously shown me only hostility and dislike, because of disagreements concerning our studies. A generous way indeed of displaying rivalry, and one worthy of a royal nature! For while friendship itself is often wont to misinterpret what is really free from faults, on this occasion keen and biting enmity was kind enough to construe in a more gentle and lenient spirit than I deserved both my mistakes, which may have been many, and my rhetorical failures, which were doubtless not a few. On this one occasion and in this one instance mad fury seemed to become sane, and by this action to free itself from the imputation of lunacy.

I am quite overcome with pride and joy at finding myself surrounded on all sides by such an assembly of learned men; and yet, when I take stock of myself and turning my eyes inward contemplate in my own heart the meagre powers I possess, I blush to myself and a sudden uprush of modesty overwhelms and chokes my rising joy.

But, gentlemen, do not, I beg of you, desert me as I lie here fallen, and stricken by your eyes as by lightning. Let the soft breeze of your goodwill refresh my fainting spirit, as well it can, and warm it into life again; so shall my sickness, thanks to you, be less acute, and the remedy, since it is you who apply it, the more willingly and gladly accepted; so that it would be a true pleasure to me often to faint thus, if I might as often be revived and restored by you. But what matchless power, what marvellous virtue is yours, which like Achilles' spear, the gift of Vulcan, at once inflicts the wound and heals it? For the rest, let no one wonder that I triumph, like one exalted to heaven, at finding so many men eminent for their learning, the very flower as it were of the University, gathered together here; for I can scarce believe that a greater number flocked of old to Athens to hear those two supreme orators, Demosthenes and Aeschines, contending for the crown of eloquence, or that such felicity ever fell to the lot of Hortensius at any declamation of his, or that so great a company of cultured men ever graced a speech of Cicero's. So that with however poor success I perform my task, it will yet be no mean honour to me merely to have opened my lips before so large and crowded an assembly of our most eminent men. And by heaven, I cannot help flattering myself a little that I am, as I think, far more fortunate than Orpheus or Amphion; for they did but supply the trained and skilful touch to make the strings give forth their sweet harmony, and the exquisite music was due as much to the instrument itself as to their apt and dexterous handling of it. But if I win any praise here to-day, it will be entirely and truly my own, and the more glorious in proportion as the creations of the intellect are superior to manual skill. Besides, Orpheus and Amphion used to attract an audience consisting only of rocks and wild beasts and trees, and if any human beings came, they were at best but rude and rustic folk; but *I* find the most learned men altogether engrossed in listening to my words and hanging on my lips. Lastly, those rustics and wild beasts used to follow after the stringed music which they already knew well and had often heard before; *you* have been drawn hither and held fast here by expectation alone.

But, Members of the University, I would before all have you know that I have not spoken thus in a spirit of boastfulness. For I only wish that such a stream of honeyed, or rather nectared, eloquence might be granted me, if but for this once, as of old ever steeped and as it were celestially bedewed the great minds of Athens and of Rome; would that I could suck out all the innermost marrow of persuasion, pilfer the note-books of Mercury himself, and empty all the coffers of wit, that I might produce something worthy of such great expectations, so notable a concourse, and so polished and refined an audience. So behold, my hearers, to what my consuming desire and longing to please you drives me and carries me away: all unexpectedly I find myself involved in an ambition which is, however, an honourable one, and a righteous sacrilege, if there can be such a thing.

Certainly I do not consider that I need beg and implore the help of the Muses, for I find myself surrounded by men in whom the Muses and the Graces are incarnate, and it seems to me that Helicon and all the other shrines of the Muses have poured forth their nurslings to celebrate this day, so that one might well believe that the laurels of Parnassus pine and fade for lack of them. Therefore it will surely be useless to seek the Muses, the Graces, and the Loves in any other spot

88

in all the world than this. If so, Barbarity, Error, Ignorance, and all that tribe which the Muses loathe must needs take flight with all speed at sight of you, and hide themselves in a far distant clime. And then, why should not every barbarous, vulgar, or mean word or phrase be forthwith banished from my speech, and I myself become straightway eloquent and accomplished, through the working of your influence and secret inspiration?

However that may be, I entreat you, my hearers, to spare a little of your time to my frivolities, for even the gods themselves are said often to have laid aside for the moment the cares of the commonwealth of heaven and to have been present as spectators of the wars of puny man. Sometimes, indeed, the stories tell, they did not disdain a humble state, but accepted the hospitality of the poor and gladly made a meal of beans and herbs. So too I beg and beseech you, my kind hearers, to accept what I can offer as in some sort a humble banquet for your delicate and discerning taste.

I am indeed well aware that many sciolists are in the habit of arrogantly and stupidly belittling in others any subject of which they happen to know nothing themselves, as if it were not worth spending trouble upon; so for instance one foolishly rails at Dialectic, because he could never master it; another despises Natural Philosophy, because, to be sure, the fairest of the goddesses, Nature, never so honoured him as to show herself naked to his eyes. But for my part I will not shrink from singing the praises of jests and merriment to the best of my powers, even though I must admit that I have but very slight aptitude for them. I must however first point out that I am to-day to praise mirth in a serious style, which seems an arduous task indeed and far from easy.

Nor are these praises undeserved. For what is more likely to win friendship quickly and retain it long, than a pleasant and gay disposition? while if a man is devoid of wit and humour and elegant pleasantry, hardly anyone will find him agreeable or welcome. But in our own case, Members of the University, if we made it our daily custom to go to sleep and so to speak die in philosophy and grow old among the thorns and brambles of logic, without any relaxation or breathing-space, what, I ask, would the pursuit of philosophy amount to but to prophesying in the cave of Trophonius and following the over-rigid rule of Cato? Why, the very rustics would say that we drank vinegar. Besides, just as those who exercise themselves in wrestling and other sports grow much stronger than others and more ready for all emergencies, even so we usually find that these mental gymnastics strengthen the sinews of the mind and tone up its whole system, and polish and sharpen the intellect, making it versatile and adaptable. But if a man does not desire to be considered cultured and witty, he must not be annoyed if he is called a clown and a boor. There is a certain mean kind of fellow, often enough met with, who, being themselves incapable of wit or gaiety, and conscious of their own dullness and stupidity, always conclude that any witty remark they may hear is made at their expense. It would indeed serve them right if their unreasonable suspicions were to be realised, and if they should find themselves the butt of everyone's witticisms, till they were almost driven to suicide. But such dregs of mankind as these cannot stand in the way of the pleasantry of polite society.

Would you now, gentlemen, have one build up a structure of proof from instances upon this foundation of reason? I can indeed find plenty of such instances. First of all comes Homer, the rising sun or morning star of cultured literature, at whose birth all learning was born also, as his twin. He sometimes withdrew his divine mind from the councils of the gods and the doings in heaven and diverted it to comic subjects, such as that most amusing description of the battle of frogs and mice. Moreover Socrates, according to the Pythian Apollo the wisest of men, is said often to have bridled his wife's shrewish tongue with a jesting word. Besides, we read that the conversation of the ancient philosophers was always sprinkled with witty sayings and enlivened by a pleasant sparkle; and it was certainly this quality above all which conferred an immortal fame upon all the ancient writers of comedies and epigrams, whether Greek or Latin. Moreover we are told that Cicero's jokes and witticisms, collected by Tyro, filled three volumes. And we are all familiar with that sprightly encomium of Folly composed by an author of no small repute, while we have many other diverting essays on comic subjects by famous authors of our own times.

Would you have me cite great generals, kings, and heroes? Take then Pericles, Epaminondas, Agesilaus, and Philip of Macedon, who, if I may speak in Gellius's manner, overflowed with humorous and witty sayings, according to the statements of historians. Take too Laelius, Scipio, Pompey, Julius Caesar and Augustus, all of whom were, according to Cicero, pre-eminent among their contemporaries for wit. Would you have yet greater names? Jove himself and the other deities are represented by the poets, who give us the best pictures of the truth, as giving themselves up to merriment at their feasts and carouses. Finally, gentlemen, I invoke the precedent and example set by yourselves, which I consider worth all the rest. For that jests and jollity are far from displeasing to you is proved clearly enough by your coming here in crowds to-day, and to this every one of you seems to nod assent. Nor, I swear, is it to be wondered at that all honest and all eminent men find pleasure in this lively and elegant pleasantry, since it too has a place of honour in the famous Aristotelian classification of virtues, and as in a common temple shines in splendour like a goddess among her sister deities.

But perhaps there may be some bearded Masters of crabbed and surly nature, who, thinking themselves Catos not merely in a small way but on a grand scale, and composing their countenances to a Stoic severity, shake their obstinate heads and uneasily complain that

91

nowadays everything is in confusion and going from bad to worse, and that the newly-created Bachelors, instead of expounding the *Prior Analytics* of Aristotle, shamelessly and unreasonably bandy about scurrilous and empty trivialities, and that to-day's exercises, which our forbears undoubtedly instituted with the proper and honest purpose of winning some solid gain either of rhetoric or of philosophy, have of late been perverted into a show of feeble witticism. But I have an answer to them ready to hand. Let them know, if they do not know already, that when the laws of our Republic of Letters were first laid down, learning had only just penetrated from foreign lands to our country; therefore, since the knowledge of Greek and Latin was exceedingly rare and unusual, it was necessary to strive and struggle toward them with the more intensive study and more unremitting efforts. We however, though inferior to our predecessors in morals, are superior to them in learning, and ought to turn our backs on those studies which offer but little difficulty, and betake ourselves to those to which they too would have turned their attention, had they had leisure to do so. And you are well aware that the earliest lawgivers were always wont to issue ordinances rather harder and more severe than men could endure, in order that as men grew less strict and accurate in their observance of them they might hit upon the right mean. Finally, since the circumstances are now entirely different, we must necessarily allow many laws and customs, if not to lapse and fall into disuse, at least to be narrowed in their application and disregarded in some details. But, they say, raising their eyebrows, if such frivolities are to be openly tolerated and approved and to win public praise, every student will straightway turn his attention away from sound and solid learning and devote it to shows and stage frivolity, so that the very training schools of philosophy will send out, instead of learned and prudent men, fellows fit only to be buffoons and play-actors.

For my part, I consider that a man who can be so given up to foolish jests as altogether to neglect for them his serious and really useful work, is incapable of distinguishing himself in either of these spheres: not in that of serious work, for if he were by nature adapted and suited to dealing with serious matters he would not, I am sure, allow himself to be so easily led away from them; nor yet in that of frivolity, because no one can be master of a fine and clever wit who has not first learnt how to behave seriously.

But I am afraid, gentlemen, that I have been spinning out my speech too long. I will not make excuses for this as I might, lest in excusing it I should aggravate my fault. In a moment we shall shake off the fetters of rhetoric and throw ourselves into comic licence. If in the course of this I outgo by a finger's breadth, as they say, my usual habits and the strict rules of modesty, I beg you, gentlemen, to accept this explanation: it is to give you pleasure that I have put off and for the moment laid aside my usual habit, and if anything I may say is loose or licentious, put it down to the suggestion, not of my real mind and character, but of the needs of the moment and the genius of the place. And so I entreat at the beginning of my entertainment the favour which actors beg at the end of theirs: give me your laughter and applause.

(ii) THE PROLUSION

At a moment when the commonwealth of fools is, as it seems, tottering and on the brink of disaster, I have been made its Dictator, though I know not how I have deserved the honour. Why should the choice fall on me, when that famous leader and commander of all the Sophisters was an eager candidate for the post, and would have fulfilled its duties valiantly; for that seasoned warrior on a previous occasion boldly led some fifty Sophisters, armed with short staves, across Barnwell Field, and, as a step toward laying siege to the town in the approved military style, destroyed the aqueduct, in order to force the townsfolk to surrender through shortage of water. I am deeply distressed at this hero's recent departure, since his going leaves all us Sophisters not merely headless but beheaded.

I ask you now to imagine, gentlemen, although it is not the first of April, that we are celebrating the Hilaria in honour of the Mother of the Gods, or a festival sacred to the god Laughter. Laugh, then, and raise a roar from your saucy lungs, smooth out the wrinkles of your brows, make a long nose if you like, but don't turn it up at anything; let the whole place re-sound with shouts of mirth, let unbridled hilarity make the tears of merriment flow freely, so that laughter may drain them dry, leaving not a drop to grace the triumph of grief. For my part, if I see anyone not opening his mouth as wide as he should to laugh, I shall say that he is trying to hide teeth which are foul and decayed, and yellow from neglect, or misplaced and projecting, or else that at to-day's feast he has so crammed his belly that he dares not put any extra strain upon it by laugh-ing, *ne praecinenti ori succinat, et aenigmata quaedam nolens affutiat sua non Sphinx sed Sphincter anus, quae medicis interpretanda, non Oedipo, relinquo; nolim enim hilari vocis sono obstrepat in hoc coetu posticus gemitus: solvant ista medici qui alvum solvunt.* If anyone does not raise his voice loud and clear enough, I shall swear that his breath is so foul and poisonous that the fumes of Etna or Avernus could not be more noisome, or at any rate that he is in the habit of eating onions or leeks so that he dare not open his mouth for fear of making his neighbours choke with his evil-smelling breath. Next, there must be no trace of that dreadful and infernal sound, a hiss, anywhere near this assembly; for if it is heard here to-day, I shall believe that the Furies and Eumenides are skulking somewhere among you, that their snakes and serpents have found their way into your bosoms, and that the madness of Athamas has come upon you.

To be sure, gentlemen, I am quite overcome with wonder and admiration at the favour you have shown me, in forcing your way through flame and fire into this place to hear me speak. For at the very threshold there stands on the one hand our fiery bull-dog, barking forth smoke to terrify us, laying about him with his blazing staff, and puffing out mouthfuls of glowing embers. On the other hand that burning and all-consuming Furnace of ours belches forth lurid flames and pours out coiling wreaths of smoke, so that it would be as easy to force one's way past him as to traverse the road to Hades, and that against the will of Pluto; and certainly Jason himself encountered no greater danger in his attempt on the fire-breathing oxen of Mars. But now, gentlemen, you may well believe yourselves to be in heaven, after having passed through purgatory, and come safe and sound out of the fiery furnace by some new miracle. I cannot think of any hero whose valour can fairly be compared with yours; for the renowned Bellerophon showed no greater courage in subduing the fire-vomiting Chimaera, nor did those valiant champions of King Arthur more easily overcome and destroy the enchantments of the flaming, fiery castle. Hence I feel justified in promising myself a choice and select audience; for if any rubbish has passed through the furnaces and penetrated to this place, I can only say that our porters are mere jack-o'-lanterns.

But how happy and how secure we are and always shall be! For at Rome it was the custom to guard the eternal fire most carefully and scrupulously, to secure the permanence of the empire; but we are ourselves guarded by living and watchful fires. Living and watchful, did I say? that expression slipped from my tongue unawares, for now that I come to think of it, they go out at the approach of dusk, and only rekindle on a fine, bright day. Still there is good hope that our House may shine once more, since none would deny that two of the greatest luminaries of the University preside over our college; yet they would not be more highly honoured anywhere than at Rome, for there Vestal Virgins would keep them aglow and alive all night long. Or, it may be, these flaming brothers might be initiated into the seraphic order. Lastly, that half-line of Virgil applies exactly to them, "They have the vital force of fire". Indeed I am inclined to believe that Horace referred to these Lights of ours, for the elder of them, as he stands among his wife and children, "shines among them all, like the moon among lesser lights". But I cannot pass over Ovid's egregious error in saying "No creatures do we know which are born of flame". For we see flitting all around us little Sparks, the offspring of this Spark of ours. If Ovid denies this, he will necessarily be casting aspersions on their mother's good name.

To return to yourselves, gentlemen. That you may not regret having taken so difficult and dangerous a journey, here is a banquet ready prepared for you! Here are tables decked with all the luxury of Persia and loaded with rarest dainties, fit to delight and captivate the palate of a very Apicius. For it is said that eight whole boars were set before Antony and Cleopatra at a banquet, but behold, before *you* are set, as a first course, fifty fatted boars which have been pickled in beer for three years, and yet are still so tough that they may well tire out even our dog-teeth. Next, the same number of excellent oxen with magnificent tails, just roasted before the door by our fiery servant; only I am afraid all the juice has gone into the dripping-pan. After them come as many calves' heads, fat and fleshy enough, but with so little brains as not to be enough for seasoning. Then again a hundred kids, more or less, but too lean, I think, from over-indulgence in the pleasures of love. We expected a few rams with fine spreading horns, but our cooks have not yet brought them from the town. If anyone prefers birds, we can provide any number of them, long fattened on dough and flour and grated cheese. First of all, a kind of bird as green in character as in plumage, which, I fancy, must have come from the same part of the world as parrots; as they always fly about in flocks and nest in the same place, they will be served up all on one dish. I would advise you to partake of them sparingly, for besides being rather underdone and lacking in solid nutriment, they are apt to produce a rash in those who eat them, if our epicure is right. Now enjoy your feast with a right good will, for here comes a dish which I can most heartily recommend, namely an enormous turkey, so fat and stout after three years' fattening that one vast dish is scarcely big enough for it, and with such a long and horny beak that it could attack an elephant or a rhinoceros with impunity; but we have cut off the beak for convenience to-day, since the creature was beginning to be a danger to young girls and to attack women, like the large apes.

This is followed by some Irish birds (of which I do not know the name but which are very like cranes in their gait and lanky figures), though as a rule they are kept for the last course. This is a novel and rare, rather than wholesome dish, and I would therefore warn you not to taste them, for they are very apt, if our epicure is right, to produce lice. I consider that they are more likely to be useful to grooms, for they are naturally lively, spirited, and prancing, so that if they are given as a clyster to lean horses they make them more lively and fleet than they would be even if they had swallowed a dozen live eels.

You see also several geese, some of this year's hatching and some older; they have a good loud quack, and are more vocal than the frogs of Aristophanes. You will easily recognise them—in fact it is a wonder that they have not already betrayed themselves by hissing, and perhaps you will hear them in a moment.

We have besides a few eggs, but they are bad eggs.

Of fruits we have only apples and medlars, and they are gallows-fruit and are not quite ripe, so that it would be better to hang them up again to ripen in the sun.

You see what we have provided, so I beg you to help yourselves to what you fancy. But I expect you will say that this banquet, like the nocturnal feasts offered by the devil to witches, is cooked without salt, and I am afraid that you will go away hungrier than you came.

I will now turn to what concerns me more closely. The Romans had their Floralia, the rustics their Palilia, the bakers their Fornacalia, and we too keep the custom of amusing ourselves as Socrates advised, especially at this season when we find ourselves released from cares and business. Now the Inns of Court have their Lords, as they call them, so showing how ambitious they are of rank. But we, gentlemen, in our desire to come as near as may be to paternity, are eager to play in pretence a part which we should not dare really to play unless in secret; even as girls are wont to invent games of weddings and births, striving to catch and hold the shadows of those things for which they long and yearn.

Why this custom should have been neglected last year I cannot imagine, unless it was because those who were to be Fathers had shown such activity in the town that the master of the ceremonies, out of consideration for the labours they had already undergone, voluntarily excused them this duty.

But, I ask, how does it happen that I have so quickly become a Father? Good heavens, what a prodigy this is, more astonishing than any recorded by Pliny! Have I slain some serpent and incurred the fate of Tiresias? Has some Thessalian witch poured magic ointment over me? Or have I been violated by some god, like Caeneus of old, and won my manhood as the price of my dishonour, that I should be thus suddenly changed from woman into man? Some of late called me "the Lady". But why do I seem to them too little of a man? Have they no regard for Priscian? Do these bungling grammarians attribute to the feminine gender what is proper to the masculine, like this? It is, I suppose, because I have never brought myself to toss off great bumpers like a prize-fighter, or because my hand has never grown horny with driving the plough, or because I was never a farm hand at seven or laid myself down full length in the midday sun; or last perhaps because I never showed my virility in the way these brothellers do. But I wish they could leave playing the ass as readily as I the woman.

But see how stupid and ill-advised they are to reproach me with a thing upon which I can most justly pride myself. For Demosthenes himself was said to be too little of a man by his rivals and opponents. Hortensius also, the most eminent orator after Cicero, was called by Torquatus a Dionysiac singing-woman. His reply was "I would rather be a follower of Dionysus than without taste, culture, or urbanity, like you, Torquatus". (But indeed as to any such nick-name as "Lord" or "Lady" I utterly reject and repudiate it; for, gentlemen, it is only in your courts and on your platforms that I have any ambition to lord it.) Who will forbid me to rejoice at so auspicious and happy an omen, and to exult at having a reproach aimed at such great men? In the meantime, as I consider all good and excellent men to be above envy, even so I hold these spiteful fellows to be so far beneath all others as not even to be worth reviling. And so I take up my *rôle* of Father and address myself to my sons, of whom I perceive a goodly number, and I see that the jolly rascals acknowledge me as their father by a furtive nod.

Do you ask their names? I should not like my sons to be given the names of various dishes, and to furnish forth a banquet for you, for that would be too like the savagery of Tantalus and Lycaon; and I will not give them the names of the parts of the body, lest you should think me the father of so many bits of men instead of whole ones; nor do I fancy calling them after the various kinds of meat, lest in my remarks I should not keep to my muttons, as the proverb says. No, I will have them called after the Predicaments of Aristotle, to indicate the nobility of their birth and the liberality of their habits; and I shall take good care, too, that all of them are promoted to some degree before I die.

As for the salt of my wit, I don't want it to be without tang, as you say of hackneyed and stale jokes, or to be the sort of thing that some wheezy old woman would spit out. At the same time I do not think that anyone will accuse my jokes of being too biting, unless he has no teeth himself and finds fault with them because they are not like his own. Certainly on this occasion I could wish that my lot were the same as Horace's, and that I were a fishmonger's son, for then I should have just the right amount of salt, and I should send you all off so nicely pickled that you would be as sorry you ever asked for a pickling as those soldiers of ours who lately managed to escape from the island of Ré.

I want to avoid being heavily sententious in my advice to you, my sons, so as not to seem to have taken more pains in educating than in begetting you. Only take care you do not turn prodigal sons, and mind you all keep off Bass, or I will disown you as bastards. Any other advice I may have to offer had best be given in our native language; and I will do my utmost to make my meaning plain.

For the rest, I must pray to Neptune, Apollo, Vulcan, and all the artificer-gods, to strengthen my ribs with wooden supports or to bind them round with iron plates. And I must beseech the goddess Ceres also, who gave Pelops a shoulder-blade of ivory, to be so good as to repair in a similar way my sides, which are nearly worn out. It is not surprising that after so much shouting and after begetting so many sons they are rather the worse for wear.

I have "dallied" (in the Neronian sense of the word) more than long enough over these things. Now I will

overleap the University Statutes as if they were the wall
of Romulus and run off from Latin into English. Lend
me attentive ears and minds, you whom such things
amuse.

(iii) LINES AT A VACATION EXERCISE

Anno Aetatis 19. *At a Vacation Exercise in the
Colledge, part* Latin, *part* English. *The* Latin
speeches ended, the English *thus began.*

Hail native Language, that by sinews weak
Didst move my first endeavouring tongue to speak,
And mad'st imperfect words with childish tripps,
Half unpronounc't, slide through my infant-lipps,
Driving dum silence from the portal dore,
Where he had mutely sate two years before:
Here I salute thee and thy pardon ask,
That now I use thee in my latter task:
Small loss it is that thence can come unto thee,
I know my tongue but little Grace can do thee:
Thou needst not be ambitious to be first,
Believe me I have thither packt the worst:
And, if it happen as I did forecast,
The daintest dishes shall be serv'd up last.
I pray thee then deny me not thy aide
For this same small neglect that I have made:
But haste thee strait to do me once a Pleasure,
And from thy wardrope bring thy chiefest treasure;
Not those new fangled toys, and triming slight
Which takes our late fantasticks with delight,
But cull those richest Robes, and gay'st attire
Which deepest Spirits, and choicest Wits desire:
I have some naked thoughts that rove about
And loudly knock to have their passage out;
And wearie of their place do only stay
Till thou hast deck't them in thy best aray;

That so they may without suspect or fears
Fly swiftly to this fair Assembly's ears;
Yet I had rather, if I were to chuse,
Thy service in some graver subject use,
Such as may make thee search thy coffers round,
Before thou cloath my fancy in fit sound:
Such where the deep transported mind may soare
Above the wheeling poles, and at Heav'ns dore
Look in, and see each blissful Deitie
How he before the thunderous throne doth lie,
Listening to what unshorn *Apollo* sings
To th'touch of golden wires, while *Hebe* brings
Immortal Nectar to her Kingly Sire:
Then passing through the Spherse of watchful fire,
And mistie Regions of wide air next under,
And hills of Snow and lofts of piled Thunder,
May tell at length how green-ey'd *Neptune* raves,
In Heav'ns defiance mustering all his waves;
Then sing of secret things that came to pass
When Beldam Nature in her cradle was;
And last of Kings and Queens and *Hero's* old,
Such as the wise *Demodocus* once told
In solemn Songs at King *Alcinous* feast,
While sad *Ulisses* soul and all the rest
Are held with his melodious harmonie
In willing chains and sweet captivitie.
But fie my wandring Muse how thou dost stray!
Expectance calls thee now another way,
Thou know'st it must be now thy only bent
To keep in compass of thy Predicament:
Then quick about thy purpos'd business come,
That to the next I may resign my Roome.

Then ENS *is represented as Father of the Prædicaments his ten Sons,*
whereof the Eldest stood for SUBSTANCE *with his Canons, which*
ENS *thus speaking, explains.*

Good luck befriend thee Son; for at thy birth
The Faiery Ladies daunc't upon the hearth;
Thy drowsie Nurse hath sworn she did them spie
Come tripping to the Room where thou didst lie;
And sweetly singing round about thy Bed
Strew all their blessings on thy sleeping Head.
She heard them give thee this, that thou should'st still
From eyes of mortals walk invisible,
Yet there is something that doth force my fear,
For once it was my dismal hap to hear
A *Sybil* old, bow-bent with crooked age,
That far events full wisely could presage,
And in times long and dark Prospective Glass
Fore-saw what future dayes should bring to pass,
Your Son, said she, (nor can you it prevent)
Shall subject be to many an Accident.
O're all his Brethren he shall Reign as King,
Yet every one shall make him underling,
And those that cannot live from him asunder
Ungratefully shall strive to keep him under,
In worth and excellence he shall out-go them,
Yet being above them, he shall be below them;
From others he shall stand in need of nothing,
Yet on his Brothers shall depend for Cloathing.
To find a Foe it shall not be his hap,
And peace shall lull him in her flowry lap;
Yet shall he live in strife, and at his dore
Devouring war shall never cease to roare;
Yea it shall be his natural property
To harbour those that are at enmity.
What power, what force, what mighty spell, if not
Your learned hands, can loose this Gordian knot?

The next QUANTITY *and* QUALITY, *spake in Prose, then* RELATION
was call'd by his Name.

Rivers arise; whether thou be the Son,
Of utmost *Tweed*, or *Oose*, or gulphie *Dun*,
Or *Trent*, who like some earth-born Giant spreads
His thirty Armes along the indented Meads,
Or sullen *Mole* that runneth underneath,
Or *Severn* swift, guilty of Maidens death,
Or Rockie *Avon*, or of Sedgie *Lee*,
Or Coaly *Tine*, or antient hallowed *Dee*,
Or *Humber* loud that keeps the *Scythians* Name,
Or *Medway* smooth, or Royal Towred *Thame*.

The rest was Prose.

7 Delivered in the College Chapel in Defence of Learning

AN ORATION

Learning brings more Blessings to Men than Ignorance

ALTHOUGH, gentlemen, nothing could give me greater pleasure and satisfaction than your presence here, than this eager crowd in cap and gown, or than the honourable office of speaker, which I have already once or twice discharged before you, I must, to be candid, confess that I scarcely ever undertake these speeches voluntarily or of my own free will; even though my own disposition and the trend of my studies make no impediment. In fact, if the choice had been offered me, I could well have dispensed with this evening's task. For I have learnt from the writings and sayings of wise men that nothing common or mediocre can be tolerated in an orator any more than in a poet, and that he who would be an orator in reality as well as by repute must first acquire a thorough knowledge of all the arts and sciences to form a complete background to his own calling. Since however this is impossible at my age, I would rather endeavour truly to deserve that reputation by long and concentrated study and by the preliminary acquisition of that background, than snatch at a false repute by a premature and hastily acquired eloquence.

Afire and aglow with these plans and notions, I found that there was no more serious hindrance or obstacle than the loss of time caused by these constant interruptions, while nothing better promoted the development and well-being of the mind, contrary to what is the case with the body, than a cultured and liberal leisure. This I believe to be the meaning of Hesiod's holy sleep and Endymion's nightly meetings with the moon; this was the significance of Prometheus' withdrawal, under the guidance of Mercury, to the lofty solitude of the Caucasus, where at last he became the wisest of gods and men, so that his advice was sought by Jupiter himself concerning the marriage of Thetis. I can myself call to witness the woods and rivers and the beloved village elms, under whose shade I enjoyed (if I may tell the secrets of goddesses) such sweet intercourse with the Muses, as I still remember with delight. There I too, amid rural scenes and woodland solitudes, felt that I had enjoyed a season of growth in a life of seclusion.

I might indeed have hoped to find here also the same opportunity for retirement, had not the distressing task of speaking been unseasonably imposed upon me. This so cruelly deprived me of my holy meditations, so tormented my mind, intent upon other things, and so hindered and hampered me in the hard and arduous pursuit of learning, that I gave up all hope of finding any peace and began sadly to think how far removed I was from that tranquillity which learning had at first promised me, how hard my life was like to be amid this turmoil and agitation, and that all attempts to pursue

Learning had best be abandoned. And so, almost beside myself, I rashly determined on singing the praise of Ignorance, since that was not subject to these disturbances, and I proposed as the theme of dispute the question whether Art or Ignorance bestowed greater blessings on its devotees. I know not how it is, but somehow either my destiny or my disposition forbade me to give up my old devotion to the Muses; indeed, blind fate itself seemed of a sudden to be endowed with prudence and foresight and to join in the prohibition. Sooner than I could have expected, Ignorance had found her champion, and the defence of Learning devolved on me. I am delighted thus to have been played with, and am not ashamed to confess that I owe the restoration of my sight to Fortune, who is herself blind. For this she deserves my gratitude. Now I may at any rate be permitted to sing the praises of Learning, from whose embrace I have been torn, and as it were assuage my longing for the absent beloved by speaking of her. This can now hardly be called an interruption, for who would regard it as an interruption when he is called upon to praise or defend the object of his affection, his admiration, and his deepest desire?

But, gentlemen, it is my opinion that the power of eloquence is most manifest when it deals with subjects which rouse no particular enthusiasm. Those which most stir our admiration can hardly be compassed within the bounds of a speech: the very abundance of material is a drawback, and the multiplicity of subjects narrows and confines the swelling stream of eloquence. I am now suffering from this excess of material: that which should be my strength makes me weak, and that which should be my defence makes me defenceless. So I must make my choice, or at least mention only in passing rather than discuss at length the numerous arguments on whose powerful support our cause relies for its defence and security. On this occasion it seems to me that my efforts must be directed entirely to showing how and to what extent Learning and Ignorance respectively promote that happiness which is the aim of every one of us. With this question I shall easily deal in my speech, nor need I be over-anxious about what objections Folly may bring against Knowledge, or Ignorance against Art. Yet the very ability of Ignorance to raise any objection, to make a speech, or even to open her lips in this great and learned assembly, is begged or rather borrowed from Art.

It is, I think, a belief familiar and generally accepted that the great Creator of the world, while constituting all else fleeting and perishable, infused into man, besides what was mortal, a certain divine spirit, a part of Himself, as it were, which is immortal, imperishable, and exempt from death and extinction. After wandering about upon the earth for some time, like some heavenly visitant, in holiness and righteousness, this spirit was to take its flight upward to the heaven whence it had come and to return once more to the abode and home which was its birthright. It follows that nothing can be reckoned as a cause of our happiness which does not somehow take into account both that everlasting life and our ordinary life here on earth. This eternal life, as almost everyone admits, is to be found in contemplation alone, by which the mind is uplifted, without the aid of the body, and gathered within itself so that it attains, to its inexpressible joy, a life akin to that of the immortal gods. But without Art the mind is fruitless, joyless, and altogether null and void. For who can worthily gaze upon and contemplate the Ideas of things human or divine, unless he possesses a mind trained and ennobled by Art and Learning, without which he can know practically nothing of them: for indeed every approach to the happy life seems barred to the man who has no part in Learning. God would indeed seem to have endowed us to no purpose, or even to our distress, with this soul which is capable and indeed insatiably desirous of the highest wisdom, if he had not intended

us to strive with all our might toward the lofty understanding of those things, for which he had at our crea-
tion instilled so great a longing into the human mind.
Survey from every angle the entire aspect of these things
and you will perceive that the great Artificer of this
mighty fabric established it for His own glory. The
more deeply we delve into the wondrous wisdom, the
marvellous skill, and the astounding variety of its crea-
tion (which we cannot do without the aid of Learning),
the greater grows the wonder and awe we feel for its
Creator and the louder the praises we offer Him, which
we believe and are fully persuaded that He delights to
accept. Can we indeed believe, my hearers, that the vast
spaces of boundless air are illuminated and adorned with
everlasting lights, that these are endowed with such
rapidity of motion and pass through such intricate revolutions, merely to serve as a lantern for base and
slothful men, and to light the path of the idle and the
sluggard here below? Do we perceive no purpose in
the luxuriance of fruit and herb beyond the short-lived
beauty of verdure? Of a truth, if we are so little able to
appraise their value that we make no effort to go beyond
the crass perceptions of the senses, we shall show ourselves not merely servile and abject, but ungracious and
wicked before the goodness of God; for by our un-
responsiveness and grudging spirit He is deprived of
much of the glory which is His due, and of the reverence
which His mighty power exacts. If then Learning is our
guide and leader in the search after happiness, if it is
ordained and approved by almighty God, and most
conformable to His glory, surely it cannot but bring
the greatest blessings upon those who follow after it.

I am well aware, gentlemen, that this contemplation,
by which we strive to reach the highest goal, cannot
partake of true happiness unless it is conjoined with
integrity of life and uprightness of character. I know,
too, that many men eminent for learning have been of
bad character, and slaves to anger, hatred, and evil

passions, while on the other hand many utterly ignorant men have shown themselves righteous and just. What of it? Does it follow that Ignorance is more blessed? By no means. For the truth is, gentlemen, that though the corrupt morals of their country and the evil communications of the illiterate have in some instances lured into wicked courses a few men distinguished for their learning, yet the influence of a single wise and prudent man has often kept loyal to their duty a large number of men who lacked the advantages of Learning. And indeed a single household, even a single individual, endowed with the gifts of Art and Wisdom, may often prove to be a great gift of God, and sufficient to lead a whole state to righteousness. But where no Arts flourish, where all Learning is banished, there you will find no single trace of a good man, but savagery and barbarity stalk abroad. As instances of this I adduce no one country, province, or race alone, but Europe itself, forming as it does one fourth of the entire globe. Throughout this continent a few hundred years ago all the noble Arts had perished and the Muses had deserted all the Universities of the day, over which they had long presided; blind illiteracy had penetrated and entrenched itself everywhere, nothing was heard in the schools but the absurd doctrines of drivelling monks, and that profane and hideous monster, Ignorance, . assumed the gown and lorded it on our empty platforms and pulpits and in our deserted professorial chairs. Then Piety went in mourning, and Religion sickened and flagged, so that only after prolonged suffering, and hardly even to this very day, has she recovered from her grievous wound.

But, gentlemen, it is, I believe, an established maxim of philosophy that the cognisance of every art and science appertains to the Intellect only and that the home and sanctuary of virtue and uprightness is the Will. But all agree that while the human Intellect shines forth as the lord and governor of all the other faculties, it guides and illuminates with its radiance the Will also, which would else be blind, and the Will shines with a borrowed light, even as the moon does. So, even though we grant and willingly concede that Virtue without Learning is more conducive to happiness than Learning without Virtue, yet when these two are once wedded in happy union as they surely ought to be, and often are, then indeed Wisdom raises her head aloft and shows herself far superior, and shining forth takes her seat on high beside the king and governor, Intellect, and gazes upon the doings of the Will below as upon some object lying far beneath her feet; and thereafter for evermore she claims as her right all excellence and splendour and a majesty next to that of God Himself.

Let us now leave these heights to consider our ordinary life, and see what advantages Learning and Ignorance respectively can offer in private and in public life. I will say nothing of the argument that Learning is the fairest ornament of youth, the strong defence of manhood, and the glory and solace of age. Nor will I mention that many men highly honoured in their day, and even some of the greatest men of ancient Rome, after performing many noble deeds and winning great glory by their exploits, turned from the strife and turmoil of ambition to the study of literature as into a port and welcome refuge. Clearly these honoured sages realised that the best part of the life which yet remained to them must be spent to the best advantage. They were first among men; they wished by virtue of these arts to be not the last among the gods. They had once striven for glory, and now strove for immortality. Their warfare against the foes of their country had been far other, but now that they were facing death, the greatest enemy of mankind, these were the weapons they took up, these the legions they enrolled, and these the resources from which they derived their strength.

But the chief part of human happiness is derived from the society of one's fellows and the formation of

friendships, and it is often asserted that the learned are
as a rule hard to please, lacking in courtesy, odd in
manner, and seldom gifted with the graciousness which
wins men's hearts. I admit that a man who is almost
entirely absorbed and immersed in study finds it much
easier to converse with gods than with men, either because he habitually associates with the gods but is
unaccustomed to human affairs and a stranger among
them, or because the mind, expanding through constant meditation on things divine and therefore feeling
cramped within the narrow limits of the body, is less
expert in the nicer formalities of social life. But if such
a man once forms a worthy and congenial friendship,
there is none who cultivates it more assiduously. For
what can we imagine more delightful and happy than
those conversations of learned and wise men, such as
those which the divine Plato is said often to have held
in the shade of that famous plane-tree, conversations
which all mankind might well have flocked to hear in
spell-bound silence? But gross talk and mutual incite-
ment to indulge in luxury and lust is the friendship of
ignorance, or rather the ignorance of friendship.

Moreover if this human happiness consists in the
honourable and liberal joys of the mind, such a pleasure
is to be found in Learning and Art as far surpasses
every other. What a thing it is to grasp the nature of
the whole firmament and of its stars, all the movements
and changes of the atmosphere, whether it strikes terror
into ignorant minds by the majestic roll of thunder or
by fiery comets, or whether it freezes into snow or hail,
or whether again it falls softly and gently in showers or
dew; then perfectly to understand the shifting winds
and all the exhalations and vapours which earth and sea
give forth; next to know the hidden virtues of plants
and metals and understand the nature and the feelings,
if that may be, of every living creature; next the delicate
structure of the human body and the art of keeping it
in health; and, to crown all, the divine might and power

of the soul, and any knowledge we may have gained concerning those beings which we call spirits and genii and daemons. There is an infinite number of subjects besides these, a great part of which might be learnt in less time than it would take to enumerate them all. So at length, gentlemen, when universal learning has once completed its cycle, the spirit of man, no longer confined within this dark prison-house, will reach out far and wide, till it fills the whole world and the space far beyond with the expansion of its divine greatness. Then at last most of the chances and changes of the world will be so quickly perceived that to him who holds this stronghold of wisdom hardly anything can happen in his life which is unforeseen or fortuitous. He will indeed seem to be one whose rule and dominion the stars obey, to whose command earth and sea hearken, and whom winds and tempests serve; to whom, lastly, Mother Nature herself has surrendered, as if indeed some god had abdicated the throne of the world and entrusted its rights, laws, and administration to him as governor.

Besides this, what delight it affords to the mind to take its flight through the history and geography of every nation and to observe the changes in the conditions of kingdoms, races, cities, and peoples, to the increase of wisdom and righteousness. This, my hearers, is to live in every period of the world's history, and to be as it were coeval with time itself. And indeed, while we look to the future for the glory of our name, this will be to extend and stretch our lives backward before our birth, and to wrest from grudging Fate a kind of retrospective immortality. I pass over a pleasure with which none can compare—to be the oracle of many nations, to find one's home regarded as a kind of temple, to be a man whom kings and states invite to come to them, whom men from near and far flock to visit, while to others it is a matter for pride if they have but set eyes on him once. These are the rewards of study, these are the prizes which learning can and often does bestow upon her votaries in private life.

What, then, of public life? It is true that few have been raised to the height of majesty through a reputation for learning, and not many more through a reputation for uprightness. Such men certainly enjoy a kingdom in themselves far more glorious than any earthly dominion; and who can lay claim to a twofold sovereignty without incurring the charge of ambition? I will, however, add this one thing more: that there have hitherto been but two men who have ruled the whole world, as by divine right, and shared an empire over all kings and princes equal to that of the gods themselves; namely Alexander the Great and Augustus, both of whom were students of philosophy. It is as though Providence had specially singled them out as examples to humanity, to show to what sort of man the helm or reins of government should be entrusted.

But, it may be objected, many nations have won fame by their deeds or their wealth, without owing anything to learning. We know of but few Spartans, for example, who took any interest in liberal education, and the Romans only admitted philosophy within the walls of their city after a long time. But the Spartans found a lawgiver in Lycurgus, who was both a philosopher and so ardent a student of poetry that he was the first to gather together with extreme care the writings of Homer, which were scattered throughout Ionia. The Romans, hardly able to support themselves after the various risings and disturbances which had taken place in the city, sent ambassadors to beg for the Decemviral Laws, also called the Twelve Tables, from Athens, which was at that time foremost in the study of the liberal Arts.

How are we to answer the objection that the Turks of to-day have acquired an extensive dominion over the wealthy kingdoms of Asia in spite of being entirely devoid of culture? For my part, I have certainly never heard of anything in that state which deserves to be regarded as an example to us—if indeed one should dignify with the name of "state" the power which a horde of utter barbarians united by complicity in crime has seized by violence and murder. The provision of the necessaries of life, and their maintenance when acquired, we owe not to Art but to Nature; greedy attacks on the property of others, mutual assistance for purposes of plunder, and criminal conspiracy are the outcome of the perversion of Nature. Some kind of justice indeed is exercised in such states, as might be expected; for while the other virtues are easily put to flight, Justice from her throne compels homage, for without her even the most unjust states would soon fall into decay. I must not, however, omit to mention that the Saracens, to whom the Turks are indebted almost for their existence, enlarged their empire as much by the study of liberal culture as by force of arms.

If we go back to antiquity, we shall find that some states owed not merely their laws but their very foundation to culture. The oldest progenitors of every race are said to have wandered through the woods and mountains, seeking their livelihood after the fashion of wild beasts, with head erect but stooping posture. One might well think that they shared everything with the animals, except the dignity of their form; the same caves, the same dens, afforded them shelter from rain and frost. There were then no cities, no marble palaces, no shining altars or temples of the gods; they had no religion to guide them, no laws or law-courts, no bridal torches, no festal dance, no song at the joyful board, no funeral rites, no mourning, hardly even a grave paid honour to the dead. There were no feasts, no games; no sound of music was ever heard: all these refinements were then lacking which idleness now misuses to foster luxury. Then of a sudden the Arts and Sciences breathed their divine breath into the savage breasts of men, and instilling into them the knowledge of themselves, gently

drew them to dwell together within the walls of cities.
Therefore of a surety cities may well expect to have a
long and happy history under the direction of those
guides by whom they were first of all founded, then
firmly based on laws, and finally fortified by wise
counsels.

What now of Ignorance? I perceive, gentlemen, that
Ignorance is struck blind and senseless, skulks at a
distance, casts about for a way of escape, and complains
that life is short and Art long. But if we do but remove
two great obstacles to our studies, namely first our bad
methods of teaching the Arts, and secondly our lack of
enthusiasm, we shall find that, with all deference to
Galen or whoever may have been the author of the
saying, quite the contrary is the truth, and that life is
long and Art short. There is nothing so excellent and
at the same time so exacting as Art, nothing more
sluggish and languid than ourselves. We allow ourselves to be outdone by labourers and husbandmen in
working after dark and before dawn; they show greater
energy in a mean occupation, to gain a miserable livelihood, than we do in the noblest of occupations, to win
a life of true happiness. Though we aspire to the highest
and best of human conditions we can endure neither
hard work nor yet the reproach of idleness; in fact we
are ashamed of owning the very character which we hate
not to have imputed to us.

But, we object, our health forbids late hours and hard
study. It is a shameful admission that we neglect to
cultivate our minds out of consideration for our bodies,
whose health all should be ready to impair if thereby
their minds might gain the more. Yet those who make
this excuse are certainly for the most part worthless
fellows; for though they disregard every consideration
of their time, their talents, and their health, and give
themselves up to gluttony, to drinking like whales, and
to spending their nights in gaming and debauchery,
they never complain that they are any the worse for it.

Since, then, it is their constant habit and practice to show eagerness and energy in the pursuit of vice, but listlessness and lethargy where any activity of virtue or intelligence is concerned, they cannot lay the blame on Nature or the shortness of life with any show of truth or justice. But if we were to set ourselves to live modestly and temperately, and to tame the first impulses of headstrong youth by reason and steady devotion to study, keeping the divine vigour of our minds unstained and uncontaminated by any impurity or pollution, we should be astonished to find, gentlemen, looking back over a period of years, how great a distance we had covered and across how wide a sea of learning we had sailed, without a check on our voyage.

This voyage, too, will be much shortened if we know how to select branches of learning that are useful, and what is useful within them. In the first place, how many despicable quibbles there are in grammar and rhetoric! One may hear the teachers of them talking sometimes like savages and sometimes like babies. What about logic? That is indeed the queen of the Arts, if taught as it should be, but unfortunately how much foolishness there is in reason! Its teachers are not like men at all, but like finches which live on thorns and thistles. "O iron stomachs of the harvesters!" What am I to say of that branch of learning which the Peripatetics call metaphysics? It is not, as the authority of great men would have me believe, an exceedingly rich Art; it is, I say, not an Art at all, but a sinister rock, a quagmire of fallacies, devised to cause shipwreck and pestilence. These are the wounds, to which I have already referred, which the ignorance of gownsmen inflicts; and this monkish disease has already infected natural philosophy to a considerable extent; the mathematicians too are afflicted with a longing for the petty triumph of demonstrative rhetoric. If we disregard and curtail all these subjects, which can be of no use to us, as we should, we shall be surprised to find how many

116

whole years we shall save. Jurisprudence in particular suffers much from our confused methods of teaching, and from what is even worse, a jargon which one might well take for some Red Indian dialect, or even no human speech at all. Often, when I have heard our lawyers shouting at each other in this lingo, it has occurred to me to wonder whether men who had neither a human tongue nor human speech could have any human feelings either. I do indeed fear that sacred Justice will pay no attention to us and that she will never understand our complaints and wrongs, as she cannot speak our language.

Therefore, gentlemen, if from our childhood onward we never allow a day to pass by without its lesson and diligent study, if we are wise enough to rule out of every art what is irrelevant, superfluous, or unprofitable, we shall assuredly, before we have attained the age of Alexander the Great, have made ourselves masters of something greater and more glorious than that world of his. And so far from complaining of the shortness of life and the slowness of Art, I think we shall be more likely to weep and wail, as Alexander did, because there are no more worlds for us to conquer.

Ignorance is breathing her last, and you are now watching her final efforts and her dying struggle. She declares that glory is mankind's most powerful incentive, and that whereas a long succession and course of years has bestowed glory on the illustrious men of old, we live under the shadow of the world's old age and decrepitude, and of the impending dissolution of all things, so that even if we leave behind us anything deserving of everlasting fame, the scope of our glory is narrowed, since there will be few succeeding generations to remember us. It is therefore to no purpose that we produce so many books and noble monuments of learning, seeing that the approaching conflagration of the world will destroy them all. I do not deny that this may indeed be so; but yet to have no thought of glory when we do well is above all glory. The ancients could indeed derive no satisfaction from the empty praise of men, seeing that no joy or knowledge of it could reach them when they were dead and gone. But we may hope for an eternal life, which will never allow the memory of the good deeds we performed on earth to perish; in which, if we have done well here, we shall ourselves be present to hear our praise; and in which, according to a wise philosophy held by many, those who have lived temperately and devoted all their time to noble arts, and have thus been of service to mankind, will be rewarded by the bestowal of a wisdom matchless and supreme over all others.

Let the idle now cease to upbraid us with the uncertainties and perplexities of learning, which are indeed the fault not so much of learning as of the frailty of man. It is this consideration, gentlemen, which disproves or mitigates or compensates for Socrates' famous ignorance and the Sceptics' timid suspension of judgment.

And finally, we may well ask, what is the happiness which Ignorance promises? To enjoy what one possesses, to have no enemies, to be beyond the reach of all care and trouble, to pass one's life in peace and quiet so far as may be—this is but the life of a beast, or of some bird which builds its little nest in the farthest depths of the forest as near to the sky as it can, in security, rears its offspring, flits about in search of sustenance without fear of the fowler, and pours forth its sweet melodies at dawn and dusk. Why should one ask for that divine activity of the mind in addition? Well, if such is the argument, we will offer Ignorance Circe's cup, and bid her throw off her human shape, walk no longer erect, and betake her to the beasts. To the beasts, did I say? they will surely refuse to receive so infamous a guest, at any rate if they are either endowed with some kind of inferior reasoning power, as many maintain, or guided by some powerful instinct,

enabling them to practise the Arts, or something re-
sembling the Arts, among themselves. For Plutarch
tells us that in the pursuit of game, dogs show some
knowledge of dialectic, and if they chance to come to
cross-roads, they obviously make use of a disjunctive
syllogism. Aristotle points out that the nightingale in
some sort instructs her offspring in the principles of
music. Almost every animal is its own physician, and
many of them have given valuable lessons in medicine
to man; the Egyptian ibis teaches us the value of
purgatives, the hippopotamus that of blood-letting.
Who can maintain that creatures which so often give us
warning of coming wind, rain, floods, or fair weather,
know nothing of astronomy? What prudent and strict
ethics are shown by those geese which check their dangerous loquacity by holding pebbles in their beaks as
they fly over Mount Taurus! Our domestic economy
owes much to the ants, our commonwealth to the bees,
while military science admits its indebtedness to the
cranes for the practice of posting sentinels and for the
triangular formation in battle. The beasts are too wise
to admit Ignorance to their fellowship and society; they
will force her to a lower station. What then? To stocks
and stones? Why even trees, bushes, and whole woods
once tore up their roots and hurried to hear the skilful
strains of Orpheus. Often, too, they were endowed with
mysterious powers and uttered divine oracles, as for
instance did the oaks of Dodona. Rocks, too, show a
certain aptitude for learning in that they reply to the
sacred words of poets; will not these also reject Ignorance? Therefore, driven lower than any kind of beast,
lower than stocks and stones, lower than any natural
species, will Ignorance be permitted to find repose in
the famous "non-existent" of the Epicureans? No, not
even there; for Ignorance must be something yet worse,
yet more vile, yet more wretched, in a word the very
depth of degradation.

I come now to you, my learned hearers, for even

without any words of mine I see in you not so much arguments on my side as darts which I shall hurl at Ignorance till she is slain. I have sounded the attack, do you rush into battle; put this enemy to flight, drive her from your porticos and walks. If you allow her to exist, you yourselves will be that which you know to be the most wretched thing in the world. This cause is the personal concern of you all. So, if I have perchance spoken at much greater length than is customary in this place, not forgetting that this was demanded by the importance of the subject, you will, I hope, pardon me, my judges, since it is one more proof of the interest I feel in you, of my zeal on your behalf, and of the nights of toil and wakefulness I consented to endure for your sakes. I have done.

COMMENTARY

[*The numerical references are to pages alone. I have referred to Masson's Life of Milton as "Masson" and to the edition of Milton's prose in the Bohn Library as "Bohn". For the first volume of Masson I have used the second edition; the other volumes did not get beyond a first edition. For matters of fact concerning the letters I have made free use of Masson, and have not always given a specific reference.*]

PREFACE

vii. The letters were translated by Robert Fellowes early in the nineteenth century and by John Hall (Philadelphia, 1829). Fellowes's translation, that given in the third volume of the Bohn Library edition of Milton's prose, is very readable but by no means reliable. Some letters may be translated accurately and elegantly; in others the sense may be distorted or difficulties completely cut. Not having the benefit of Masson's researches Fellowes frequently goes wrong over proper names. Hall's volume is rare. Here again the translation is cultured but inaccurate. But Hall knew more about Milton and the circumstances in which the letters were written than Fellowes did. One or two of his notes I have found useful. Francis Peck in his *New Memoirs of the Life and Poetical Works of Mr John Milton* (London, 1740) gives an awkward version of the *Second Prolusion*. Masson in his *Life of Milton* gave a new version of all the letters and translated for the first time large portions of the *Prolusions*. Though perhaps more accurate than Fellowes and Hall, Masson's versions offend by their style, which mingles floweriness with the jargon which in his day only too often resulted from a training in word-for-word translation from the classics. For instance he turns the words "omnium Artium omnisque Scientiae circulari quodam subsidio instructum et consummatum" into "instructed and finished with a certain circular subsidy of all the arts and all science".

INTRODUCTION

ix. *Textually...it is the original edition only that counts.* This statement must be explained or qualified. The manuscripts of two of the letters published in the 1674 volume have survived: nos. 10 and 11, to Carlo Dati and Hermann Mylius. I do not know where the first is, but the first sentence and the closing

121

words are given in facsimile by J. F. Marsh, *Papers connected with the Affairs of Milton*, frontispiece (Chetham Society Publications, 1851), and by Sotheby, *Ramblings in the Elucidation of the Autograph of Milton* (1861), p. 122. The second letter (one of the least important) is preserved in the state archives at Oldenburg. The facsimile in Marsh and Sotheby shows some slight differences from the printed text. But even if the complete manuscript were available, I should not depart from the printed edition, which must have been issued under Milton's direction, unless compelled by obvious error.

xi. *Urbanity...in the* De Doctrina Christiana. Bohn, v, 125.

xiii. *The seventh letter, to Diodati.* For discussion of this letter see J. H. Hanford, *Youth of Milton* (University of Michigan Publications, Language and Literature, 1), pp. 144 ff.; and E. M. W. Tillyard, *Milton*, p. 382.

xv. *This is the mood of* Paradise Regained. See my *Milton*, p. 306, for further explanation.

xvi. *Our knowledge of what Cambridge was like.* Masson in the first volume of his *Life of Milton* and J. Bass Mullinger in his third volume of *The University of Cambridge* have written independent studies of Cambridge in Milton's day, based on the original documents. I have made free use of both these volumes.

xvii. *Barnwell Field.* One of the two areas of common arable land belonging to Cambridge before the Enclosure Acts. Cambridge was peculiar in having two fields. See Arthur Gray, *The Town of Cambridge*, p. 18:

The curious feature about Cambridge is that it had two, each an agricultural unit cultivated on the three-field system. The Field on the northern and western sides of the town was called Cambridge Field; that on the southern and eastern sides was generally known as Barnwell Field....The duplicate Field seems to have its origin in a twofold community.

xix. For the quotation from Bacon's *Advancement of Learning*, see the Spedding-Ellis-Heath edition of Bacon, iii, 285.

xx. For Bacon's letter to the University see *Letters and Life of Bacon*, vii, 438–9.

xxvii-xxviii. For notes on the Platonic and Aristotelian references see pp. 137–8 below.

xxxv. *At the end of the autobiographical passage in the* Defensio Secunda. See Bohn, i, 258–9.

12. *Eskimos.* (Literally, "Hyperboreans".) Diodati was in medical practice somewhere in the north of England. The beginning of the next letter refers to Diodati's medical profession.

"*The dream of a shade*": σκιᾶς ὄναρ. Pindar, *Pythian Odes*, VIII, 136.

Letter 7. *To* CHARLES DIODATI

For comment on this letter see above, p. xiii.

14. "*For many forms there are of things divine*": πολλαὶ μορφαὶ τῶν δαιμονίων. A phrase used at the close of several plays of Euripides, *Bacch.* 1388, *Andr.* 1285, *Hel.* 1688, *Alc.* 1159.

My plan is to take rooms in one of the Inns of Court. Milton here shows himself to be tiring of the isolation of Horton. His immediate intention of living in London was diverted by his journey to Italy.

15. *This stepmotherly warfare.* Diodati's father had recently married again.

Letter 8. *To* BENEDETTO BUONMATTEI

15. *Buonmattei*, born in 1581, was a priest and one of the most important scholars in Florence when Milton visited it. He was a great authority on the Italian language, and the treatise to which Milton refers, *Della Lingua Toscana*, was published in Florence in 1643 (see Masson, I, 778–9).

16. *When the language falls into corruption and decay, etc.* The idea that there is a direct connection between the state of a language and national morality is very typical of the Renaissance in general and of Milton in particular. Culture and action or morals were closely associated in Milton's mind.

18. *Fabius*: i.e. Quintilian, who gives a summary description of classical writers in the tenth book of his *De Institutione Oratoria*.

Letter 9. *To* LUCAS HOLSTENIUS

19. Lucas Holstenius or Lukas Holste, a naturalised Roman of German extraction, was Librarian of the Vatican. This letter was written during Milton's second visit to Florence. Between the two visits he had been to Rome and made Holstenius's acquaintance.

Cherubini was a precocious Roman scholar who died at the age of 28.

The souls in Virgil. Aeneid, VI, 679:

—penitus convalle virenti
inclusas animas superumque ad lumen ituras.

20. *Cardinal Francesco Barberini* was Prime Minister of Rome and protector of the interests of England and Scotland at the Papal Court.

Public concert. It was here probably that Milton heard the great singer, Leonora Baroni, to whom he addressed three Latin epigrams.

Codex Mediceus. A fifth century MS. of Virgil.

Doni was a Florentine scholar, then on a visit to Rome.

21. *Callimachus said of Ceres. Hymn to Demeter,* 58:

῎Ιθματα μὲν χέρσῳ, κεφαλὰ δέ οἱ ἅψατ᾽ Ὀλύμπῳ.

Letter 10. *To* CARLO DATI

22. *Dati* was a younger man than Milton, aged 18 when they met at Florence. He was a prominent member of the learned societies there and had besides an international reputation. He achieved some fame by his book on the lives of the ancient painters, published 1667.

Your unexpected letter. An unpublished draft of a letter of Dati to Milton is, I hear, to be published in the Columbia edition of Milton. I do not know if the draft is of this letter.

Soon an even more depressing thought, etc. Here Milton refers to the presence in his house of his first wife's family, the Powells. Ruined by the Royalist defeat at Naseby and by the fall of Oxford in June, 1646, they sought refuge with Milton in London. He was generous in housing them, but, as the present letter shows, he did not enjoy their company.

Either by death.... Milton may be thinking of Diodati, but also of his own father, who died earlier in this year.

23. *Tomb of Damon.* Damon is Diodati. Diodati knew, Milton means, how much Milton loved Italy. The elegy is the *Epitaphium Damonis,* on Diodati, written by Milton shortly after he returned from Italy. Lines 125 to 138 refer to his Italian friends. He mentions Dati by name:

Quin et nostra suas docuerunt nomina fagos
Et Datis, et Francinus; erant et vocibus ambo
Et studiis noti, Lydorum sanguinis ambo.

COMMENTARY

24. *Any of my poems that are in Latin.* The 1645 edition of
Milton's poems contained both English and Latin.

Harsh expressions about the Pope. The reference is to *In
Quintum Novembris,* where the Pope is made the instigator of
the Gunpowder Plot.

Your description of King Louis' funeral. Dati was known in
France and was later in favour with Louis XIV. The reference here is to the death of Louis XIII on May 14th, 1643,
which Dati seems to have celebrated.

Coltellini, Francini, etc. For Milton's Florentine friends see
Masson, I, 772–87.

Letter 11. *To* HERMANN MYLIUS

25. *Mylius* was envoy of the Count of Oldenburg sent to
treat for a commercial agreement with the Commonwealth. He
had been introduced to Milton and had asked him to use his influence to expedite the business of the treaty. The request of the
Count was granted early in February, 1652, by which the
present letter can be dated (see Masson, IV, 416–7, 424).

This letter is one of seven written by Milton to Mylius, the
originals of which are preserved in the state archives at Oldenburg. The other six are short business letters of trifling importance. The last to remain unknown was published recently by
Mr Thomas O. Mabbott in *Notes and Queries,* September 20th,
1930, p. 208. For discussion of others, see letter from Mr Mabbott in *Times Literary Supplement,* February 16th, 1928.

Poor health. Milton was exhausted by the strain of writing
his reply to Salmasius, the *Defensio pro Populo Anglicano,* and of
his growing blindness now nearly complete. (For his state of mind
at this period see my *Milton,* pp. 187–91.) In view of Milton's
troubles his zeal for his friend's cause is remarkable.

Removal to another house. From Scotland Yard to "a pretty
garden house, in Petty France in Westminster...opening into
St James's Park" (Phillips, *Life of Milton*). Later this house was
known as 19 York Street, Westminster, and was occupied by
Jeremy Bentham and Hazlitt.

Mr Frost. Secretary of the Council of State, the executive
body of the Commonwealth.

The President. At this time Sir Arthur Haselrig.

Letter 12. *To* LEONARD PHILARAS

For comment see Introduction above, p. xi.

26. *Philaras.* Born at Athens near the end of the sixteenth century, he had been educated in Italy, and had experience of war and diplomacy as well as of scholarship. He enjoyed the patronage of Richelieu and was well known in Paris under the name of Villeré (Masson, IV, 444–5).

Augier. René Augier, formerly Resident Agent in Paris for the English Parliament.

27. *Re-awaken in the hearts of the Greeks the courage, etc.* Milton doubts whether the Greeks are fit for liberty. In his study of history, Milton had concluded that only the virtuous can bear liberty, and that slavery is usually deserved. He utters this thought more than once in his works. "Liberty sought out of season, in a corrupt and degenerate age, brought Rome itself to a farther slavery" (*History of Britain*, Bohn, V, 239):

> But what more oft in Nations grown corrupt,
> And by thir vices brought to servitude,
> Then to love Bondage more than Liberty?
>
> (*Samson Agonistes*, 268–70).

See too the splendid passage in *Defensio Secunda* (Bohn, I, 295–6).

Letter 13. *To* RICHARD HEATH

27. *Richard Heath.* Nothing is known of him beyond what this letter tells us. He must have been an early pupil of Milton. At this date he was a clergyman.

Letter 14. *To* HENRY OLDENBURG

28. *Oldenburg*, a Saxon, was agent for the city of Bremen with the Commonwealth. He came to London shortly before this date and ended by making England his country. He later studied at Oxford, was tutor to Richard Jones (later Lord Ranelagh), and became a member and Fellow of the Royal Society.

29. *"Defence"*: the *Defensio Secunda*, published in the spring of 1654.

"Cry to Heaven" refers to the anonymous *Regii Sanguinis Clamor ad Caelum* written in answer to the first *Defensio*. Milton wrote his *Defensio Secunda* against it.

Some doubt as to his identity. Milton thought that Alexander More, or Morus as he was commonly called, was the author, but

did not keep back his treatise when this attribution was found
to be doubtful. See Aubrey's statement:

His sharp writing against Alexander More, of Holland, upon a mistake,
notwithstanding he had given him by the Dutch ambassador all satisfaction to the contrary: viz. that the booke called *Clamor* was writt by
Peter du Moulin. Well, that was all one; he having writt it, it should
goe into the world; one of them was as bad as the other.

My handling of the subject-matter. Oldenburg, though ap-
proving of Milton's pamphlet as a whole, seems to have objected
to its tone. Milton had indeed attacked Morus's personal character with violence. It would seem too from what follows that
Oldenburg had tried to persuade Milton to drop the controversy
and turn his attention to other things. He was not successful, as
Milton wrote the *Pro Se Defensio* before settling down finally
to *Paradise Lost.* But Milton makes it very clear how much he
disliked controversy, although he attached an enormous importance to it.

30. *Far different and more delightful occupations.* I have no
doubt that Milton was thinking of poetry and *Paradise Lost*
when he says *delightful* ("Me vero primum *dulces* ante omnia
Musae", wrote Virgil in a passage Milton was to imitate in his
hymn to light at the beginning of Book Three of *Paradise Lost*).
For this passage in Milton's letter as evidence for his taking up
Paradise Lost at this time see my *Milton*, pp. 194–6.

Letter 15. *To* LEONARD PHILARAS

This letter is the chief authority for diagnosis of the cause of
Milton's blindness. For the latest discussion of this see Dr Arnold
Sorsby's excellent article "On the Nature of Milton's Blindness"
in *British Journal of Ophthalmology*, 1930, pp. 339–54.

The courageous tone of this letter is exactly that of the sonnet
to Cyriack Skinner on his blindness.

30. *Many look down upon me.* Milton had been proud of his
physical fitness, and must have felt blindness to be a physical
humiliation.

31. *Description in the* Argonautica. Apollonius Rhodius,
Argonautica, II, 205 (Seaton's translation).

Letter 16. *To* LEO DE AITZEMA

32. *Leo de Aitzema*, or Lieuwe van Aitzema, formerly agent
for Hamburg and the Hanseatic Towns in London, where he
must have got acquainted with Milton, now held the same posi-

tion at the Hague. He had written to Milton concerning a proposed translation into Dutch of one of Milton's writings on divorce. Milton here writes an answer to this letter.

Letter 17. *To* EZEKIEL SPANHEIM

33. *Ezekiel Spanheim*, at this time aged 25, was destined to be famous as scholar, antiquary, and diplomat. Both he and his father, Frederick (now dead, but once Professor of Theology at Geneva), were enemies of Morus, Milton's object of attack in the *Defensio Secunda* (see Masson, v, 171–2). Ezekiel must have written to Milton about his controversy with Morus, furnishing him with new material against their common enemy.

34. *Calandrini*: a member of an Italian family of merchants, settled in Geneva.

My defence of myself is the *Pro Se Defensio*, to be published in August, 1655.

Letter 18. *To* RICHARD JONES

Masson (v, 267) has pointed out that this letter, which is the twenty-second in the printed edition, is in its wrong place. All the other letters are in the proper order, which is chronological. This letter has been inserted in its proper place here, and the necessary renumbering carried out.

35. *Richard Jones* was afterwards Viscount Ranelagh. He had been a pupil of Milton and now, about May, 1656, he was at Oxford under the tutorship of Oldenburg (see above, p. 128). Lady Ranelagh, his mother, was an intimate friend of Milton at this time. She was a Boyle, and like several of that family an intellectual. Her son was now about sixteen.

The place to which you have now retired: Oxford. The end of the sentence expresses Milton's inveterate dislike of the education given at the Universities. See the next letter also.

Like a second Timothy. See 2 *Tim.* i, 5:

When I call to remembrance the unfeigned faith that is in thee, which dwelt first in thy grandmother Lois, and thy mother Eunice; and I am persuaded that in thee also.

Letter 19. *To* HENRY OLDENBURG

Written to Oldenburg at Oxford.

36. *Young Ranelagh*: Richard Jones, to whom the previous letter was addressed. See note to that letter.

The Jesuit Martini was a missionary to China.

Cyriack: Cyriack Skinner, who had been one of Milton's pupils.

Letter 20. *To* RICHARD JONES

37. *She has supplied the place of every family tie.* Milton
married his second wife, Katherine Woodcock, in November of
this year, that is, about two months after writing this letter. In
this retrospective reference to his obligations to Lady Ranelagh
he may be thinking of his forthcoming marriage.

You extol the victories of princes. It is doubtful of what
military prowess Jones had been speaking, but it is like Milton
to condemn *mere* military success. To be worth anything it must
be preceded by self-mastery in the soldier. See the last pages of
the *Defensio Secunda*, and the characters of Cromwell and Fair-
fax in the same work. One of the morals of *Samson Agonistes* is
the same. Samson in his humiliation exclaims:

> But what is strength without a double share
> Of wisdom?

In the country of mutton-heads. A reference to Juvenal, x, 50,
Vervecum in patria. There is no reason to suspect with Masson
some hidden political meaning. Milton's quotation has nothing
to do with the context from which it is taken; its function is to
add picturesqueness to the idea that in the actual rough-and-
tumble of war stupid people may be very successful.

Letter 21. *To* PETER HEIMBACH

38. *Peter Heimbach.* Little is known of him. He was a young
Dutchman or German who had known Milton in London and
was now in Holland.

Letter 22. *To* EMERIC BIGOT

39. *Emeric Bigot* was a French scholar born in 1626. He
corresponded with various scholars abroad and must have met
Milton on a visit to England.

Sight...not so much lost as retired and withdrawn into myself.
Compare Milton's reference to his blindness in *Paradise Lost*,
III, 51–3:

> So much the rather thou Celestial light
> Shine inward, and the mind through all her powers
> Irradiate, there plant eyes.

He writes in the same way about his blindness and its com-
pensation, in *Defensio Secunda* (Bohn, I, 239).

39. *Telephus*, King of Mysia, in repelling the attack of the Greeks on that country, was wounded by Achilles. The wound proving incurable, he enquired of an oracle, and being told that only he who inflicted the wound could ease it, at length persuaded Achilles, who cured him by means of the rust of the spear which had wounded him.

40. *Book on the manner of holding Parliaments.* Masson annotates:

It seems to me possible that the book...was one entitled *Modus tenendi Parliamentum apud Anglos*, by Henry Elsynge, Clerk of the House of Lords....The book, which had been sent forth under Parliamentary authority in 1641, was a standard one; and manuscript copies of it, or drafts for it, more complete than itself, may well have been extant in such places as the Cotton Library or Bradshaw's. (Masson, v, 285 n.1.)

The following Byzantine histories. For the books to which Milton refers see Masson, v, 285–6.

Mr Stoupe: a French Swiss, once a minister to a French church in London, now a government agent in secret missions to France and Switzerland.

Letter 23. *To* HENRY DE BRASS

See Introduction above, p. xii.

41. *Henry de Brass.* Masson has no information to give about him. Milton's letter shows that he was a young foreigner on his travels. We know that about this time Milton was much sought out by foreign visitors.

At the opening of the Catiline. Sallust, *Catiline*, III, 2.

42. *One who would be a worthy historian.* Milton sets the historian the same exacting standard he had set the epic poet in the *Apology for Smectymnuus*:

He who would not be frustrate of his hope to write well hereafter in laudable things, ought himself to be a true poem; that is, a composition and pattern of the best and honourablest things; not presuming to sing high praises of heroic men, or famous cities, unless he have in himself the experience and the practice of all that which is praiseworthy.

The province of the politician. After his high hopes of a regenerate England at the beginning of the Civil War, Milton gradually conceived a dislike of politicians and a doubt of the value of reforms politically achieved. Such a dislike can be detected in *Paradise Regained*. See my *Milton*, pp. 120–4, 159, 175–6, 306.

Sallust...extolled Cato. Sallust, *Catiline*, LIV, 5: "At Catoni studium modestiae, decoris, sed maxume severitatis erat". This, however, refers to Cato's character as a man rather than as a writer.

Letter 24. *To* HENRY OLDENBURG

43. *Saumur.* Oldenburg was now accompanying Richard Jones in France, as his tutor.

Charon's boat...Charenton boat, etc. Oldenburg had told Milton the news that Morus, his old enemy, had been appointed minister of the church of Charenton, one of the chief Protestant churches in France, frequented by the Protestants of Paris. The meaning of the pun (one of Milton's worst) seems to be that the news was bad and Milton wishes he had not heard it. A ghost on Charon's boat, about to drink the waters of forgetfulness, was of all creatures the least likely, having heard it, to have communicated it. Charenton is close to Paris, on the Seine. Hence the reference to the boat.

Horace. This and the following quotation are from Horace, *Epist.* i, 13, 4–8 (Wickham's translation).

44. *Lawrence.* Henry Lawrence, the younger, Milton's pupil. Milton addressed a sonnet to him.

Letter 25. *To* RICHARD JONES

This letter, bearing the same date, was presumably sent along with the last. It is the most priggish letter Milton wrote; one can only hope that it was a pure formality, Milton feeling that he does not wish to write to Oldenburg without also writing to his charge.

Letter 26. *To* HENRY DE BRASS

45. *Quintilian. Inst. Or.* X, 1, 112: "ille se profecisse sciat, cui Cicero valde placebit".

Aristotle. Rhet. III, 17, 1418a: γνώμαις δὲ χρηστέον καὶ ἐν διηγήσει, καὶ ἐν πίστει· ἠθικὸν γάρ.

Letter 27. *To* PETER HEIMBACH

For comment on this letter, which tells us something about Milton's relations with the Council of State, see Masson, V, 381–2.

46. *Your letter dated...December 18th.* By contemporary English reckoning the date would be December 8th.

Letter 28. *To* JEAN LABADIE

47. *Jean Labadie,* born 1610, Jesuit, mystic, heretic, Protestant Minister at Orange and Utrecht, and founder of a sect called the Labadists. Milton seems to have looked on him as a serious Protestant crusader rather than as the charlatan he undoubtedly was. He probably knew little about him, but that did not prevent his espousing his cause with zeal.

Durie. John Durie was a Scotsman, well known in Europe, who had a great scheme for uniting all the Protestant churches. He translated Milton's *Eikonoklastes* into French.

Du Moulin. Peter Du Moulin, now a very old man. A distinguished French Protestant theologian. Father of the Du Moulin who was the real author of *Regii Sanguinis Clamor,* wrongly assigned by Milton to Morus.

Letter 29. *To* HENRY OLDENBURG

Milton writes in the midst of the confusion that preceded the Restoration. Oldenburg and Richard Jones were still abroad in France.

49. *I hope that God will not permit.* Milton kept on hoping, against all probability, that the ruin of his political hopes would not be consummated by the return of Charles.

Protestant Synod of Loudun. A Synod of the French Protestant churches which was held at Loudun in Anjou from November 10th, 1659 to January 10th, 1660.

Synod…in which Nazianzen took part. The reference is to the second Oecumenical Council, convoked by Theodosius in Constantinople in 381. Gregory Nazianzen was president of the Council, but was unable to control it.

Posthumous adversary. Salmasius had at his death left an unpublished manuscript answering Milton's *Defensio pro Populo Anglicano.*

Letter 30. *To* RICHARD JONES

This letter is more obviously formal than letter twenty-five. It looks as if Milton was not interested in Richard Jones, but felt himself bound to write to him when he wrote to Oldenburg. Possibly he wrote to please Jones's mother, Lady Ranelagh.

50. *The roads to vice and to virtue.* It is possible, as Hall pointed out, that this letter owes something to the little Greek philosophical allegory, the *Pinax* of Cebes. Milton knew Cebes,

as he mentions him in his *Tractate on Education*. Cebes insists on mere learning being common to both virtue and vice; and Milton is thinking of learning when he speaks of the "pleasant and flowery road common to both". The "steep and rugged ascent which leads to virtue alone" is close to Cebes's ἀνοδία τραχεῖα καὶ πετρώδης that leads to the hill of true discipline.

Letter 31. *To* PETER HEIMBACH

For comment on this, the one letter written after the Restoration, see Introduction above, p. xv.

51. *A refuge for me in the country*: Chalfont St Giles, where Ellwood found him a cottage.

ACADEMIC EXERCISES

First Academic Exercise

Whether Day or Night is the more excellent

53. *How can I hope for your good-will?* For Milton's relations with his fellow-undergraduates see above, pp. xxi–xxii.

"Polydamas and the women of Troy prefer Labeo to me". Persius, *Satires*, I, 4–5. Those who are curious to know the various possible references in this passage must seek them in an annotated Persius. Attius Labeo had made a very bad translation of Homer. Persius's lines are in part taken from *Iliad*, XXII, 100 and 105, where Hector says he is ashamed not to face Achilles for fear of what Polydamas and the Trojan women might say. Polydamas had previously criticised Hector's strategy. In Persius Polydamas would stand for a critic, the women of Troy for the emasculate Roman audience, and Labeo for a bad poet. It's all one to him if a bad critic and a worthless audience prefer a rotten poet to him. The application of Persius's lines to Milton's case is as obvious as it is uncomplimentary to his audience.

54. *A serpent's slough*. An adaptation of the Greek proverb quoted by Athenaeus (VIII, 362b): σαυτὸν δ᾽ ἀποφαίνεις κενότερον λεβηρίδος—"You show yourself emptier than a serpent's slough".

Frogs of Seriphus. According to the belief current in classical times, the frogs on the island of Seriphus did not croak. See Aelian, *Hist. Anim.* III, 37, and Pliny, *N.H.* VIII, 227. They

COMMENTARY

were said to have been struck dumb by Zeus, at the prayer of
Perseus, who, during his pursuit of the Gorgon, wished to sleep
but was disturbed by their croaking. It was suggested that their
dumbness was due to the coldness of the water, or to the fact that
they were really not frogs at all but toads; Aelian and Pliny,
however, both insist that they were able to croak when transported elsewhere.

56. *Hesiod...in the line "From Chaos"*, etc. *Theogony*, 123.

Hesiod, whom I have ... quoted. Ibid. 124–5.

58. *Greek name of* εὐφρόνη. Εὐφρόνη really means "the
kindly time". Milton here seems to take the meaning as
"sensible".

Martial. Ep. VIII, 35. Milton quotes this as:

> Uxor pessima, pessimus maritus,
> Non miror bene convenire vobis.

The last line has been altered to suit the context, and should read
Miror, non bene convenire vobis—"I wonder that you do not
agree well together".

Tel arbre, tel fruit. The nearest modern equivalent to the
Greek proverb quoted by Milton, κακοῦ κόρακος κακὸν ᾠόν—
"a bad crow lays a bad egg".

Democritus' notions. At first sight it seems strange that Milton
should thus assume the absurdity of the theory put forward by
Democritus. It had, however, been discredited first by Aristotle's
insistence on the doctrine of causes (whereas according to Democritus there was no real cause except blind chance) and later
through its adoption by the Epicurians.

60. *Orpheus...in his hymn to Dawn.* Orphic *Hymn to Dawn*,
XXVIII, 7–11.

62. *Canidia* was a lady attacked by Horace in his *Epodes*
(3, 5, and 17) as ugly and a witch.

The groans of spectres, the screeching of owls, etc. As Milton
is usually taken very literally and seriously it may be well to
point out the obvious, namely that the whole of the description
of the horrors of night is burlesque. It thus fits the quasi-comic
tone of the rest of the *Prolusion*.

Second Academic Exercise

On the Harmony of the Spheres

On the Pythagorean and Platonic doctrine of celestial music see the very interesting pamphlet of the English Association, *The Greek Strain in English Literature*, by Professor J. Burnet. Milton is not so well informed as Professor Burnet, in that he attributes to Pythagoras and Plato the notion that the planets were fixed on spheres. This notion is later than Plato. "The doctrine of Pythagoras", wrote Professor Burnet, "was that the Sun, the Moon, and the five planets then known, with the heaven of the fixed stars, formed a scale or octave, the intervals of which were numerically determined by the distances between the orbits." Plato in the vision of Er at the end of the *Republic* elaborated the idea by placing a Siren in each of the planetary orbits, who sings in monotone her proper note in the octave. Aristotle (*De Caelo*, II, 9, 290*b*) quite briefly dismisses the notion of a symphony of sound as fantastic and false. He records the objection that no one has ever actually heard the planetary music. It is these brief Aristotelian passages which Milton tries to answer.

For an account of the way in which this *Prolusion* is developed see Introduction above, pp. xxvii–xxviii.

65. *The golden chain suspended by Jove.* Homer, *Il.* VIII, 18 ff., where Zeus proposes to prove his superiority to the other gods by letting down a golden chain to the earth, asserting that they will not be able to drag him down, whereas he will be able to draw the earth up to heaven.

Leaf, in a note on the passage, says: "It is curious that this line, which evidently alludes to a mere trial of strength…should have been made the base of all sorts of mystical interpretations and esoteric myths from the earliest times. Thus in Plato we find, *Theaetetus*, 153*c*, τὴν χρυσῆν σειρὰν ὡς οὐδὲν ἄλλο ἢ τὸν ἥλιον Ὅμηρος λέγει….A collection of similar far-fetched allegories will be found in Eustathius, *ad loc.* The neo-Platonists took up the idea, and from them it was handed on to the alchemists of the Middle Ages, in whose mystical cosmogony the *aurea catena Homeri* signified the whole chain of existences up to the *quinta essentia universalis*".

Aristotle…those Intelligences of yours. According to the astronomic theory of Aristotle, the "Unmoved Mover" directly causes the motion of the sphere of the fixed stars, that of the

COMMENTARY

remaining spheres being due to the action of divine beings or subordinate gods presiding over each sphere. Donne uses the notion several times, *e.g.* in the *Extasie*, 49–52:

> But O alas, so long, so farre
> Our bodies why doe wee forbeare?
> They are ours, though they are not wee, Wee are
> The intelligences, they the spheare.

66. *The fault is in our own deaf ears.* Cf. *Arcades*, 72–3,

> The heavenly tune, which none can hear
> Of human mould with grosse unpurged ear.

For a discussion of the music of the spheres in Milton's early thought see my *Milton*, pp. 375–8.

Aristotle...those goats you tell of. Aristotle, *Meteor.*, 1, 4, 341 *b*, mentions lights in the sky popularly called "torches" or "goats".

67. *As Persius says.* Satires, II, 61: "O curvae in terris animae et coelestium inanes".

Third Academic Exercise

An Attack on the Scholastic Philosophy

For general comment see Introduction above, pp. xxii–xxiv.

68. *Cave of Trophonius.* Trophonius was a Boeotian hero worshipped at Lebadea. He had an oracle in a cave there. Milton's phrase implies oracular obscurity.

72. *Twist the rope in Hades in company with...Ocnus.* The curious legend of Ocnus, who continually twisted a rope which an ass devoured as fast as he made it, is well known in classical literature and art. Apparently it merely symbolises misdirected effort, though other interpretations have been put forward.

Fourth Academic Exercise

In the Destruction of any Substance there can be no Resolution into First Matter

73. *Sons of Earth:* giants.

Ovid's well-known poem...Astraea. Ovid, *Metamorphoses*, 1, 150: "ultima caelestum terras Astraea reliquit". Astraea was the last of the immortals to leave the earth at the end of the Golden Age.

138

74. *The goddess Lua.* An early Italian goddess, to whom the arms taken from a defeated enemy used to be dedicated, but whose worship had already been forgotten in classical times. Her name has sometimes been connected with *luo* and taken to mean "the deliverer".

Lipsius, an eminent Belgian scholar, 1547–1606.

78. *Philoponus,* of Alexandria, lived in the seventh century A.D., and wrote commentaries on Aristotle.

Fifth Academic Exercise

There are no partial Forms in an Animal in addition to the Whole

83. *Chrysostom Javello.* A Dominican monk (born *c.* 1471) esteemed as a philosopher and theologian.

Sixth Academic Exercise

(i) THE ORATION

Sportive Exercises on occasion are not inconsistent with philosophical Studies

85. *Ship of Fools:* Sebastian Brandt's *Narrenschiff* (1494), known in England from Barclay's version *The Ship of Fools* (1508).

86. *Democritus.* See note on p. 136.

Junius Brutus. Roman Consul on the expulsion of Tarquinius Superbus and his family from Rome. *Lusts of kings* refers to the rape of Lucretia.

Disagreements concerning our studies. See above, p. xxii.

87. *Achilles' spear.* See note on p. 132 (Telephus.)

Hortensius. A famous Roman orator, rival of Cicero.

89. *Did not disdain a humble state.* The Latin is *humiles non dedignati casus, et paupere hospitio excepti.* Possibly (with Masson) *casas* (homes) should be read for *casus* (states), but there is no absolute need to change the text.

90. *Prophesying in the cave of Trophonius.* For Trophonius see above, p. 138. Milton seems to mean by the phrase, doing

nothing but spin out oracular responses away from all contact with the world outside.

91. *Author of no small repute:* Erasmus.

Gellius: author of the *Noctes Atticae,* a miscellany of history, anecdote, etc.

(ii) THE PROLUSION

93. *Sophisters.* Students in their last year before taking the B.A. degree.

Barnwell Field. See above, p. 122.

95. *Flame and fire.* Here begins a long series of puns on the names of two college servants. Dr A. H. Lloyd, of Christ's College, who kindly offered to see if traces of these men existed in the college records, has identified one of them. In the college accounts for alternate years between 1626 and 1632 he found the item "Sparks his liverey 1. o. o." Dr Lloyd writes:

I think this points to the porter who, of all the college servants, is the person to be garbed in something approaching splendour, as he represents the dignity of the college in the eyes of the extra-mural world. The sum of one pound in those days would be equal to a sum so much greater now as to make one, though reluctant to supply an exact figure as multiplier, certain that it was at least adequate to the task of providing a very creditable livery.

One can well imagine the delight with which Milton's undergraduate audience would hail his jokes about so outstanding a college figure.

Whether the second man was actually a brother of this Sparks, as the phrase "these flaming brothers" might suggest, is uncertain. He may merely chance to have had an equally convenient name, such as Coles or Furness; the latter is suggested by the repeated mention of a furnace.

Jason himself encountered no greater danger. The text has *minori cum periculo,* when for the sense *majori* is required. It has been assumed that Milton made this simple slip, and *majori* has been substituted in the translation.

96. *That half-line of Virgil. Aeneid,* VI, 730: "Igneus est ollis vigor".

That Horace referred to these Lights of ours. Epodes, XV, 1–2.

> Nox erat, et caelo fulgebat Luna sereno
> Inter minora sidera.

To return to yourselves, gentlemen. It is impossible to make out the references in what follows. Classes of undergraduates and individuals are referred to under various guises.

Apicius. A noted Roman epicure.

97. *Bad eggs.* κακοῦ κόρακος—"of a bad crow". See note on p. 136 on this Greek proverb, for which the nearest suitable pun has been substituted.

98. *Gallows-fruit. Infelicis arboris*—"of an evil tree", a Latin euphemism for the gallows.

Cooked without salt. It is impossible to bring out in English the double meaning of the Latin *sal*, "salt" and "wit".

The Inns of Court have their Lords. Milton is speaking of the names given to the masters of the revels. At the Inns of Court they are *Domini*; at Cambridge they are *Patres*. Milton, the "Father" of the present entertainment, goes on to make jokes about his paternity.

Tiresias. The story of Tiresias's change of sex is told by Ovid in *Metamorphoses*, III, 316 ff. Once, seeing two serpents together, he killed the female. Whereupon he changed his sex. Seven years later he again saw two serpents, killed the male, and changed his sex again. Tiresias, then, was an authority on the differences of the sexes. Mr T. S. Eliot has revived the legend in *The Waste Land.*

Caeneus. The text, uncorrected hitherto, reads *Cnœeus*, a misprint for *Caeneus.* Caenis, daughter of Elatus of Thessaly, was Poseidon's paramour. The god being unfaithful to her, she persuaded him to turn her into a man—Caeneus. In Virgil's Hades she has regained her original sex (Ovid, *Metamorphoses*, XII, 189 ff.; Virgil, *Aeneid*, VI, 448–9).

Some of late called me "the Lady". The present passage is not our only source for Milton's nickname at Christ's. Aubrey mentions it.

99. *But indeed as to any such nick-name as " Lord" or " Lady".* The argument here is a little difficult to follow. This sentence looks like an impatient interruption of the argument. "Indeed", he says, "I don't want to be a 'superior person', at all, except in the courts of academic disputation." Then he reverts in the next sentence to what had preceded the parenthesis by saying, "still it *is* a good omen to be associated with Cicero and Hortensius".

Tantalus and Lycaon. Tantalus cut up his son Pelops,

boiled him, and offered him to the gods as a meal. Lycaon sacrificed a child on the altar of Zeus.

100. *Meat...muttons.* "Nec ad vinorum genera eos nuncupare volupe est, ne quicquid dixero sit ἀπροσδιόνυσον et nihil ad Bacchum." The pun on wine and "nothing to do with Bacchus" (i.e. "not to the point") cannot be rendered literally.

Predicaments of Aristotle. From their training in scholastic philosophy Milton's audience would be entirely familiar with these. Milton is "Ens", or Being, the father of the Predicaments or Categories, which are Substance, Quantity, Quality, Relation, Action, Passion, Place, Time, Posture, and Habit.

Horace,...a fishmonger's son. A piece of gossip recorded by Suetonius.

Those soldiers of ours who lately managed to escape from the island of Ré. In 1627 Buckingham had landed on the island of Ré, on the pretext of offering help to the inhabitants of La Rochelle, and as a measure of war against France. The expedition was a failure from the beginning, and after some months the French succeeded in landing and forcing the English to abandon the attempt.

Mind you all keep off Bass, or I will disown you as bastards. This wretched pun is an attempt to represent "liberique mei ne colant Liberum, si me velint patrem".

In the Neronian sense of the word. Suetonius (*Nero*, XXXIII, 1) relates that it was a favourite witticism of Nero's that Claudius "had ceased to linger among mortals", pronouncing the word *morari* "to linger, delay", as *mōrari* "to play the fool", a pun for which no English equivalent offers itself.

(iii) LINES AT A VACATION EXERCISE

Milton now speaks as Ens, father of the Predicaments.

Seventh Academic Exercise

*Learning brings more Blessings to Men
than Ignorance*

For discussion of many points in this *Prolusion* see Introduction above, pp. xxxii–xxxix.

105. *Hesiod's holy sleep.* Hesiod (*Theogony*, 22 ff.) tells how the Muses came to him as he was watching his flocks, and bestowed upon him the gift of song.

COMMENTARY

111. *But if such a man once forms a worthy and congenial friend-ship, there is none who cultivates it more assiduously.* Compare this with the deliberate cultivation of the friendship with Diodati spoken of in letter seven. See J. H. Hanford, *Youth of Milton*, pp. 144 ff.; E. M. W. Tillyard, *Milton*, p. 382. It is interesting that this *Prolusion* long ante-dates the letter.

That famous plane-tree. The scene of Plato's *Phaedrus* is laid under a plane-tree outside the walls of Athens.

116. *O iron stomachs of the harvesters!* Horace, *Epodes*, III, 4: "O dura messorum ilia" (Wickham's translation).

117. *We live under the shadow of the world's old age.* Whether or not the world was in an advanced stage of decay was a subject of speculation in Milton's day. Milton, from his lines, "Naturam non pati Senium", seems to have been among the optimists. See my *Milton*, p. 26.

119. *The Egyptian ibis.* It is interesting that Milton, with all his zeal for the new philosophy, should relapse in this passage to the natural history of an earlier age.

Geese which check their dangerous loquacity. See Gosson, *Schoole of Abuse*,

Geese are foolish birdes, yet when they flye ouer the mount *Taurus*, they shew greate wisedome in their own defence: for they stop their pipes full of grauel to auoide gagling, and so by silence escape the Eagles.

The famous "non-existent" of the Epicureans. It was a dictum of Epicurus that "nothing springs from that which is not"— οὐδὲν γίγνεται ἐκ τοῦ μὴ ὄντος (letter of Epicurus, Diogenes Laertius, x, 38); cf. Lucretius, I, 150: "Nullam rem e nilo gigni divinitus unquam".

TEXTUAL NOTES

THE edition of 1674 contains a long list of *errata*, which, however, is far from complete. The following list contains further obvious corrections. In addition to these, the quotations from Greek authors invariably contain mistakes, which are however not enumerated here, as they can readily be checked by comparison with any standard edition. No attempt has been made to indicate changes in the punctuation, since these are too numerous, the punctuation throughout being completely at random and frequently obscuring the sense.

Page in 1674 edition

65 for *delinitum* read *delenitum*
73 for *supramodum* read *supra modum*
74 for *Amasio* read *amasio*
77 for *Clysie* read *Clytie*
79 for *emorerentur* read *emorirentur*
80 for *autumnat* read *autumat*
85 for *suasisset* read *suasissent*
107 for *captant* read *captam*[1] (?)
119 for *casus* read *casas*[2] (?)
120 for *sis* read *sit*
123 for *nimis* read *mimis*
126 for *Euminides* read *Eumenides*
127 for *minori* read *majori*[3] (?)
128 for *deliniat* read *deleniat*
129 for *pertriennalem* read *per triennalem*
131 for *Patilia* read *Palilia*
131 for *Cnæeus* read *Caeneus*[4]
141 for *industriâ* read *industria*
147 for *arreptâ potentiâ* read *arrepta potentia*

[1] *Captam* gives much better balance and antithesis, and avoids the awkward change of tense from *captant* to *traxissent*.
[2] See note on p. 139.
[3] See note on p. 140.
[4] See note on p. 141.

CAMBRIDGE: PRINTED BY W. LEWIS, M.A., AT THE UNIVERSITY PRESS